VOICES OF THE RAINBOW

Illustrations by R. C. Gorman and Aaron Yava

Also edited by Kenneth Rosen THE MAN TO SEND RAIN CLOUDS

Voices of the Rainbow

the Rainbow

EDITED BY KENNETH ROSEN

Contemporary Poetry by Native Americans

ARCADE PUBLISHING · NEW YORK

ARCADE PUBLISHING • NEW YORK

FIRST ARCADE PAPERBACK EDITION 1993

First published in hardcover as A Richard Seaver Book /The Viking Press in 1975 by The Viking Press, Inc. First paperback edition published by Seaver Books in 1980.

Library of Congress Cataloging-in-Publication Data

Voices of the rainbow : contemporary poetry by Native Americans / edited by Kenneth Rosen. — 1st Arcade pbk. ed.
       p.   cm.
  ISBN 1-55970-224-9
  1. American poetry — Indian authors. 2. Indians of North America
  — Poetry. 3. American poetry — 20th century. I. Rosen, Kenneth
  Mark, 1938–
  PS591.I55V65   1993
  811'.54080897 — dc20   93-8517

Published in the United States by Arcade Publishing, Inc., New York, by arrangement with Seaver Books, New York
Distributed by Little, Brown and Company

10 9 8 7 6 5 4 3 2 1

BP

PRINTED IN THE UNITED STATES OF AMERICA

The rainbow raised up with me.
Through the middle of broad fields,
The rainbow returned with me.
To where my house is visible,
The rainbow returned to me.

—Navajo

ACKNOWLEDGMENTS

Although most of the poems in this book have never been published before, some initially appeared in magazines and earlier collections. I am particularly grateful to Mark Vinz for permission to reprint the following poems from *Dacotah Territory 6* (Special Native American Issue, Guest Edited by James L. White): "North To Milwaukee," "Raising The Flag," "Seven Woodland Crows," and "Anishinabe Grandmothers" by Gerald Vizenor; "Eye Of God," "Earth," and "Week-Seek" by Jim Tollerud; "Wishes" and "Death" by Ya-Ka-Nes; "E Uni Que A The Hi A Tho, Father" and "Swamp" by Roberta Hill. Professor Vinz edits one of the finest poetry magazines currently being published in this country, and I welcome the opportunity to thank him for his aid and encouragement in this project.

While the contributors themselves hold the copyrights to the rest of the poetry in this collection, I acknowledge with appreciation the earlier printing of a few of the poems in the following works: *Chicago Review, Nimrod, The Haiku Anthology* by Cor Van den Heuvel, *From The Belly of The Shark* by Walter Lowenfels, *Southwest Review, Indian Historian, Poet, Voices of WahKon-Tah* by Dodge and McCullough, and *Southern Poetry Review*.

To Brother Benet Tvedten of Blue Cloud Abbey, James L. White, and Richard Hugo I offer my sincere thanks for the help they gave me in locating and contacting several of the poets represented here. To William Witherup, Jim McGrath, and Joseph Bruchac III, fine poets all, I offer my gratitude for their honesty.

CONTENTS

Gerald Vizenor   (*Minnesota Chippewa*)

Janet Campbell Hale   (*Coeur d'Alene*)

Lance Henson   (*Cheyenne*)

Contents

Anna Walters   (*Pawnee/Oto*)

Carter Revard   (*Osage*)

Contents

xii

Contents

xiv

Contents

xv

Ray A. Young Bear   (*Mesquaki*)

taste me,
I am the wind
touch me,
I am the lean gray deer
running on the edge of the rainbow.
—Leslie Marmon Silko

This collection of contemporary poetry written by American Indians is an attempt to introduce both Indian and non-Indian readers to the various worlds of immediately felt experience which we may have been unaware of or which we may have lost sight of in our haste to be done with the present moment and to move on to the next. The poems in this book, most published here for the first time, represent a collective voice, a voice that articulates a belief in the value of the past as that which has the ability to shape the present and to decide the future. But a poem is, to begin with, a very individualistic thing, and the reader will find that the works in this book also represent single voices, some of them even unique, that employ a wide variety of styles and tones.

My criteria for selection have been simple. If the reader listens carefully, can he or she hear, clearly and directly, the voice of the poet? If the reader is open to new and even strange worlds, does the poem bring one's feelings and emotions into play as well as one's intellect? While I prefer to think of American Indian literature as an integral part of literature in general, I recognize in these poems a pervasive feeling for the spiritual that resides in the palpable; a common feeling for the land, the climate, the specific place infuses this poetry with a transcendence that comes only from an artist's complete involvement in the direct imaginative response. The poets represented here offer us the sounds and shapes of a particular locale, whether it be the starkly beautiful mesas of the Southwest or the harsh details of an urban bar, and they draw from this sense of place, from this traditional sense of belonging, a feeling for something that goes beyond both individual time and individual space.

Crucial to this transcendent notion seems to be the general assumption in these poems that memory and past experience are somehow holy, sacred, to be handled with care. Regardless of the nature of the action in the past, it is treated as an essential part of the struggle to give meaning to the present and to create hope for the future. Whether it be the advice given long ago by an older member of the family or the memory of a violent and near-fatal confrontation between a Native American and an Anglo outside a saloon, the real value of the event seems to be inherent in its being remembered in the present. The sense of history is a profound one in these poems.

Important, too, is the assumption made in many of these poems that one function of today's Native American poet is carefully to present the violent reality without losing sight of the peaceful ideal. If the essential legacy passed on to Native Americans is an organic or symbiotic view of existence, then one must define oneself in terms of one's relationship to those other things in nature, both animate and inanimate. This self-definition, conducted as it is within the structure of such a worldview, necessarily entails a ritualistic approach, which often leads to violent confrontation with the majority. There are numerous examples of this confrontation in this collection, but what seems to me to be more revealing is the large number of poems that have a yea-saying tone in the midst of violence; poems that exhibit a certainty on the part of the poet about who he or she is, that stand as a testament to the value of a strong sense of self in a world that is given to fragmentation, doubt, and violence.

The twenty-one poets included in this collection represent tribal affiliations from various parts of the country: Laguna Pueblo, Colville, Sioux, Coeur d'Alene, Makah, Quapaw, Cherokee, Cheyenne, Osage, Chippewa, Pawnee/Oto, Santo Domingo Pueblo, Oneida, Nez Percé, Seneca/Seminole, Mohawk, Yaqui, Choctaw, Mesquaki, and Blackfeet. These seven women and fourteen men offer lyrical answers to the question an Indian leader once asked of a now obscure president of the United States: What visions are offered that will cause today's children to want tomorrow to come? In the case of some of these poets the visions are drawn from a deeply emotional response to their natural surroundings. For others the images are created out of a context that is almost wholly the work of the fictive imagination. In both instances, however, the picture we get is one of possibility, of something bound to be better because it couldn't get much worse, of an awareness of history that reveals a condition of harmony and individual dignity that once obtained and that may now have a chance to exist again. In some of these poems the chance appears to be a slim one, but it appears, and the vision is invariably worth contemplating.

For some readers it may be helpful to place these poems on the oral/written continuum so central to Native American literature in general, and to its poetry in particular. These works represent relatively recent pieces recorded on that band, but if you listen closely you can still hear the old singer's refrain, the incremental repetition that served as so powerful an aid to the memories of so many generations, and you can still discern the communal beat beneath the varied tones and tempos of the individual artists who now sign their names to their individual efforts. There may seem to be a great deal of distance between the Navajo Blessing Way chants and a contemporary poem about the confrontations at Wounded Knee, but it's really not so very far to go.

Finally, why a book of these particular poems? Because, as works growing out of both a strong sense of tradition and a highly individualistic sense of the creative imagination, they, in the proverbial words of the mountain climber, are there — and because I believe all Americans can benefit from direct exposure to the various worlds of the Native American that these poems offer.

When I wrote the original preface to this book almost two decades ago, Leslie Marmon Silko had not yet written *Ceremony* or *Almanac of the Dead*, Gerald Vizenor had not yet written *Bearheart: The Heirship Chronicles*, *The Heirs of Columbus*, or *Griever: An American Monkey King in China*, and Janet Campbell Hale had just published *The Owl's Story* but had yet to write *The Jailing of Cecelia Capture*. It may be a bit of a stretch for some readers, but I believe these prose works have emerged, directly or indirectly, out of the poetry you will find in this collection. To fully understand the darker threads of Silko's latest tapestry we might first try to follow the lighter ones so carefully and intricately woven into her earlier celebrative poems; to a greater or lesser extent, the same can be said of many of the poets represented here.

The latest evidence of the renewed diversity and vitality of contemporary Native American literature must include the works of N. Scott Momaday, James Welch, Louise Erdrich, Michael Dorris, Paula Gunn Allen, Linda Hogan, and Louis

Owens, but without the various voices raised in this and Duane Niatum's early collection, there would be a great deal less for these writers to build upon. If I listen carefully enough, I can still hear, clearly and directly, the voice of each of these poets. I hope you can too.

Kenneth Rosen
Taos, 1993

VOICES OF THE RAINBOW

Roberta Hill

(WISCONSIN ONEIDA)

WINTER BURN

When birds break open the sky, a smell of snow
blossoms on the wind. You sleep, wrapped up
in blue dim light, like a distant leaf of sage.
I drink the shadow under your ear
and rise, clumsy, glazed with cold.
Sun, gleaming in frost, reach me.
Touch through the window this seed that longs
little by little to flare up orange and sing.
Branches turn to threads against the sun.
Help us to wake up, enormous space that makes
us waver, dark horizon that keeps us strong.

Your heart pours over this land, pours over memories
of wild plum groves,
laughter, a blur between leaves.
These fences hold back frost, let horses run.
Spirits hunt our human warmth
in these quiet rooms. Dogs follow us,

bark at the piercing air. I sort beans,
wish for something neither key nor hand can give.
I must watch you suffering the doubt and grace
of foxes. Let clear winter burn away my eyes.
Let this seed amaze the ground again.

Beside barrels, a mouse glares at me,
folding against the present like a draft against a flame.
Curious bitter eyes tick away
my years. Women have always heard this,
his rattle signaling a day brought wide
like slow ripples in a river.
Ask him why water drifts over moss.
Your hair grows fish-haunted. You never are warned.
Ask why those waving weeds steal what you become.
His answer, the slow tick of fire.
Near timber, axes sing inside the poles.

You chop the wood and chop a buried city
from your bones. Far off, the clouds are floating into dusk.
We stack up logs, traveling to the dry field
of our breath. Like ants, we pace the ground,
and let a strange heat shake our darkness,
an old web streams through the door.
Hushed steps follow you to valleys,
where, aching and ringing, you no longer want to look,
until, touching the sudden pulse of all we are,
you burn into the yellow grass of winter,
into one reed, trembling on the plain.

BLUE MOUNTAIN

for Richard Hugo

West of your door, Blue Mountain dreams of melting
to the sea. You wait a simple answer.
Tomorrow is a harvest.
I understand what roads you've climbed
in the tinted smoke of afternoon.
Crickets whir a rough sun into haze.
The thickly planted field invades your longing.

I left that mountain, easy in good-byes.
The moon flooding me home. The Garnet Range
like arms letting go moments
when too much talk grows fatal. Now
moss folds down in matted sleep. Watch
how wind burns lazily through maples.
I sweep and sweep these broken days to echoes.

More than land's between us. Wood smoke in the sun.
Timber shrinks below the bend.
Our walls stay thin. We trust them.
We like the light to bleed around the shade.
Peepers show us why we live astonished
at new frost. You taught me how to track
this ragged fire. Chickadees keep me going.

I've begged a place for you to come at last.
Clouds gather like mints. Warm, dancing like gnats
in sunshine, rain hugs your heavy arms. Your woman smiles.
The flint lake brightens. In the slow roll
of a wave, joy buries its weight deep
inside your lungs. One bird calls from a far-off pine.
You and Blue Mountain will reach the sea.

ROBERTA HILL

3

STEPS

Digging earth from puddles, she would wake stranded.
Hollyhocks flooded the back step. Morning bright with leaves.
In green schoolrooms, chalk bit blackboards.
Robins paced the blowing grass.
Picnic day, her father sat, muttering: "She's dead,"
over and over to fresh rain.
His shoulders bent, broken like a doll.

The cow lay wrapped in drops like a bursting pear,
Mica schist. Children ran through the ponds
under ferns. Its neck was a home for midges; its smell,
a bleach for dingy clouds. In radiant sheets of water,
a shadow buried the sun.

Weeds grew to stone. She hid among witch hazels,
the yellow flowers a tired beacon.
Night air flashed on empty fields. Twice Minona teased their birth,
dotting the broken hay with footprints.
A flame danced through birches. Lights along the backbone.
Veins stuffed with stars. This life forbids comfort, traces
with fingers a terrible sharing. Years. Years to find
the right step.

Men stroked her thighs, tried to make her sleep.
Their throats went dry from calling, as ducks
caught in a thicket cry. Woolen mud never wakens,
yet bright maples gather pain.
The sap glistens, beads in moon wash.

Pretend these mountains are not hungry. I've heard a young voice
muttering at wind, like straw on fire.
She moves drunk toward lightning,
letting her arms stiffen, wanting to be fog,

the smell of dead fruit. I've covered her tracks
with a difficult river, and like a plover,
wade from water to rock and back. It foams beryl green
in the sunset, and at every bend, leaves something behind.

SWAMP

Tamaracks swing light away,
dote on slag among the clouds.
Their wavering eyes kiss, then curve
around a dog whose garbled throat
swills my night, tears my day.
I turn to bite his velvet nerve,
but find frogs instead. Sharp
like iron under skin, they try
to bleed my leather crimes, to whisper,
"Joy is tough like hide." "Surprise
them with a rock," I cry, "bruise
them down to proper size."
My red belief lies curled in mud.
A soft hot star hugged by the sea.

E UNI QUE A THE HI A THO, FATHER

White horses, tails high, rise from the cedar.
Smoke brings the fat crickets,
trembling breeze.
Find that holy place, a promise.
Embers glow like moon air.

ROBERTA HILL

5

I call you back from the grasses.
Wake me when sandpipers
fly. They fade,
and new sounds flutter. Cattails at sunrise.
Hair matted by sleep.

Sun on the meadow. Gray boughs lie tangled.
The ground I was born to
wants me to leave.
I've searched everywhere to tell you
my eyes are with the hazels.

Wind swells through fences, drones a flat ache for hours.
At night, music would echo
from your womanless bedroom.
Far down those bleaching cliffs,
roses shed a torrent.

Will you brush my ear? An ice bear sometimes lumbers west.
Your life still gleams, the edges melting.
I never let you know.
You showed me, how under snow and darkness,
the grasses breathe for miles.

SEAL AT STINSON BEACH

She asked brown eyes, "Burn me loose.
Unmask this loss of estuaries, lamp shells."
The lowland wheat dreams against moonlight
and empty houses creak their own tough joy.
On this wintry coast, remember how, in faint light,
mother's eyes wore green, how
Eleanor sank. A trunk along flat pine.

Beyond breakers, a mute hunter floats, forgetful
of running sharks, sea moss. Teach me
your crisscross answer
to the cackling of gulls.
Closets can mend
sinister days, yet these losses hum
in the walls.

He swam a shadow, a blemish on the waves.
Is this the last year of tasting dust,
of violent wakings?
Blue seashot boils around my shoes. Breakers crash.
Hiss again. He leans, foreign as a star,
for places where the man-of-war
hangs its tendrils down.
In the drawing back, the breathing in, I find my bones.

Leslie Marmon Silko

(LAGUNA PUEBLO)

WHERE MOUNTAIN LION
LAY DOWN WITH DEER   (*February 1973*)

I climb the black rock mountain
   stepping from day to day
          silently.
I smell the wind for my ancestors
    pale blue leaves
    crushed wild mountain smell.
Returning
  up the gray stone cliff
  where I descended
          a thousand years ago.
Returning to faded black stone
  where mountain lion lay down with deer.
It is better to stay up here
        watching wind's reflection
        in tall yellow flowers.
The old ones who remember me are gone
    the old songs are all forgotten

and the story of my birth.
How I danced in snow-frost moonlight
distant stars to the end of the Earth,
How I swam away
in freezing mountain water
narrow mossy canyon tumbling down
out of the mountain
out of deep canyon stone
down
the memory
spilling out
into the world.

WHEN SUN CAME TO RIVERWOMAN
(*June 10, 1973*)

that time
in the sun
beside the Rio Grande.

voice of the mourning dove
calls
long ago   long ago

remembering the lost one
remembering the love.

Out of the dense green
eternity of springtime
willows rustle in the blue wind
timeless

LESLIE MARMON SILKO

9

                    the year unknown
                        unnamed.
The muddy fast water
  warm around my feet
  you move into the current slowly

      brown skin   thighs
      deep   intensity
      flowing water.
Your warmth penetrates
                        yellow sand and sky.
Endless eyes shining always
      for green river moss
      for tiny water spiders.
Crying out   the dove
                        will not let me forget
      it is ordained
      in swirling brown water
                        and it carries you away,
                        my lost one
                        my love,
                              the mountain.
man of Sun
        came to riverwoman
        and in the sundown wind
    he left her
              to sing
                    for rainclouds swelling in the northwest sky
                    for rainsmell on pale blue winds
                              from China.

LOVE POEM   (*late spring Navajo Nation, 1972*)

Rain smell comes with the wind
　　　　　　　out of the southwest.
Smell of sand dunes
　　　　　tall grass glistening
　　　　　　　　in the rain.
Warm raindrops that fall easy
　　　　　　　　(this woman)
The summer is born.
Smell of her breathing new life
　　　　　　　small gray toads on damp sand.
(this woman)
　　　　whispering to dark wide leaves
　　　　white moon blossoms dripping
　　　　　　　　tracks in the sand.

Rain smell
　　　I am full of hunger
　　　deep and longing to touch
wet tall grass, green and strong beneath.

This woman loved a man
and she breathed to him
　　　　　　her damp earth song.

I am haunted by this story
I remember it in cottonwood leaves
　　　　　　　their fragrance in the shade.
I remember it in the wide blue sky
when the rain smell comes with the wind.

POEM FOR MYSELF AND MEI:
ABORTION   (*Chinle to Fort Defiance, April 1973*)

1

The morning sun
            coming unstuffed with yellow light
            butterflies tumbling loose
            and blowing across the Earth.
They fill the sky
            with shimmering yellow wind
            and I see them with the clarity of ice
            shattered in mountain streams
                        where each pebble is
                        speckled and marbled
                            alive beneath the water.

2

All winter it snowed
mustard grass
and springtime rained it.

Wide fancy meadows
warm green
            and butterflies are yellow mustard flowers
                        spilling out of the mountain.

3

There   were horses
    near the highway
    at Ganado.
And the white one
            scratching his ass on a tree.

4

They die softly
against the windshield
and the iridescent wings
        flutter and cling
                all the way home.

DEER SONG   (*March 7, 1974*)

1

Storm winds carry snow
to the mountain stream
clotted white in silence,
pale blue streak under ice
to the sea.
The ice shatters into glassy
bone splinters that tear deep into
soft parts of the hoof.
Swimming away from the wolves
before dawn
        choking back salt water
        the steaming red froth tide.

2

It is necessary.
Reflections that blind
from a thousand feet of
gray schist
        snow-covered in dying winter sunlight.
The pain is numbed by the freezing,
        the depths of the night sky,
        the distance beyond pale stars.

LESLIE MARMON SILKO

13

Do not think that I do not love you
if I scream
                    while I die.
Antler and thin black hoof
smashed against dark rock—
                    the struggle is the ritual
shining teeth tangled in
          sinew and flesh.

You see,
          I will go with you,
Because you call softly
Because you are my brother
          and my sister
Because the mountain is
our mother.
I will go with you
because you love me
while I die.

TOE'OSH: A LAGUNA COYOTE STORY
(for Simon Ortiz)

1

In the wintertime
at night
we tell coyote stories

                    and drink Spañada by the stove.

How coyote got his
ratty old fur coat

bits of old fur
the sparrows stuck on him
with dabs of pitch
that was after he lost his proud original one in a poker game.
Anyhow, things like that
are always happening to him
that's what she said.

And it happened to him at Laguna
and Chinle
and at Lukachukai too,
because coyote
got too smart for his own good.

2

But the Navajos say he won a contest once.
It was to see who could sleep out in a
snowstorm the longest
and coyote waited until chipmunk badger and skunk were all
curled up under the snow
and then he uncovered himself and slept all night
inside
and before morning he got up and went out again
and waited until the others got up before he came
in to take the prize.

3

Some white men came to Acoma and Laguna a hundred years ago
and they fought over Acoma land and Laguna women and
even now
some of their descendants are howling in
the hills southeast of Laguna.

4

Charlie Coyote wanted to be governor
and he said that when he got elected
he would run the other men off
the reservation
and keep all the women for himself.

5

One year
the politicians got fancy
at Laguna.
They went door to door with hams and turkeys
and they gave them to anyone who promised
to vote for them.
On election day all the people
stayed home and ate turkey
and laughed.

6

The Trans-Western pipeline vice president came
to discuss right-of-way.
The Lagunas let him wait all day long
because he is a busy and important man.
And late in the afternoon they told him
to come back again tomorrow.

7

They were after the picnic food
that the special dancers left
down below the cliff.
And Toe'osh and his cousins hung themselves
down over the cliff
holding each other's tail in their mouth

making a coyote chain
until someone in the middle farted
and the guy behind him opened his
mouth to say, "What stinks?" and they
all went tumbling down, like that.

8

Howling and roaring
Toe'osh scattered white people
out of bars all over Wisconsin.
He bumped into them at the door
until they said,
                    "Excuse me"
And the way Simon meant it
was for 300 or maybe 400 years.

ALASKAN MOUNTAIN POEM #1

(*January 1974*)

*

Dark branches
dark leaves
snow deep,
in sky
that encloses the mountain.
The sun is hidden
in green moss feathers
that cling to
the gray alder branches.

LESLIE MARMON SILKO

17

* *

On the mountain
within the endless
white sky
spruce trees entangle the snow
and only the silence
dances free.

* * *

By the time
I wrote the spruce tree poem
the snow winds came
And the mountain
was gone.

POEM FOR BEN BARNEY

(early spring Navajo Nation, 1973)

If the time ever came
I would call you
                    and you would come.
To stand on that mountain
          on top of that mountain in the West.
And I would go to the east
          stand on the mountain in the East
          and from our mountaintops
                    call them.

The meadows and mountains
the winds of the earth
     dancing   spinning   whirling
all wrapped in leather tongues.

Voices of the Rainbow

One legged antelope in the treetop swaying
Crow with his chorus singing
                    It has finally come to this
                    All their fine magic
                    It has finally come to this.
Crow and his chorus gesturing
                         at the world around them
          keeping time to Coyote's drum.

Yet so long as we can summon together
          with flute song flying in the wind
          and flute man coming from the distances
                    the instrument heavy in his hands
                    skinsoft tree in flower,
          leaping and dancing lightly
          sunshine not yet ended
                         sunshine not yet through.

FOUR MOUNTAIN WOLVES

(Chinle, late winter, 1973, when the wolves came)

I

Gray mist wolf
          from mountain frozen lake
traveling southwest
                    over deep snow crust   singing
                              Ah ouoo
                              Ah ouoo
               the fog hangs belly high
               and the deer have all gone.
                    Ah ouoo
                    Ah ouoo

LESLIE MARMON SILKO

Lonely for deer gone down to the valley
Lonely for wild turkey all flown away.
                              Ah ouoo
                              Ah ouoo

Gray mist wolf
                following the edge of the Sun.

                              2
Swirling snow wolf
  spill the yellow-eyed wind
                                    on blue lake stars
                                          Orion
                                                Saturn.
Swirling snow wolf
                tear the heart from the silence
                rip the tongue from the darkness.
                Shake the earth with your breathing
                and explode gray ice dreams of eternity.

                              3
Mountain white mist wolf
        frozen crystals on silver hair
        icy whiskers
                        steaming silver mist from his mouth.
Gray fog wolf
                silent
        swift and wet
                        howling along cliffs of midnight sky,
        you have traveled the years
                        on your way to Black Mountain.

Call to the centuries as you pass
                howling wolf wind

their fear is your triumph
they huddle in the distances
                                            weak.

Lean wolf running
        where miles become faded in time,
        the urge   the desire   is always with me
        the dream of green eyes wolf
        as she reaches the swollen belly elk
                softly
        her pale lavender outline
        startled into eternity.

SLIM MAN CANYON
                    (*early summer Navajo Nation, 1972*)
                    (*for John*)

700 years ago
        people were living here
        water was running gently
        and the sun was warm
                on pumpkin flowers.
It was 700 years ago
        deep in this canyon
        with sandstone rising high above
The rock   the silence   tall sky and flowing water
        sunshine through cottonwood leaves
        the willow smell in the wind
                                700 years.
The rhythm
        the horses' feet   moving strong through
                                white deep sand.

LESLIE   MARMON   SILKO

Where I come from is like this
    the warmth, the fragrance, the silence.
Blue sky and rainclouds in the distance
    we ride together
        past cliffs with stories and songs
        painted on rock.
            700 years ago.

PRAYER TO THE PACIFIC

1

I traveled to the ocean
    distant
        from my southwest land of sandrock
        to the moving blue water
    Big as the myth of origin.

2

Pale
pale water in the yellow-white light of
        sun floating west
          to China
        where ocean herself was born.
Clouds that blow across the sand are wet.

3

Squat in the wet sand and speak to Ocean:
    I return to you turquoise the red coral you sent us,
        sister spirit of Earth.
Four round stones in my pocket I carry back the ocean
        to suck and to taste.

4

Thirty thousand years ago
            Indians came riding across the ocean
            carried by giant sea turtles.
Waves were high that day
            great sea turtles waded   slowly   out
                        from the gray sundown sea.
Grandfather Turtle rolled in the sand   four times
                        and disappeared
                                    swimming into the sun.

5

And so   from that time
            immemorial,
                        as the old people say,
rainclouds drift from the west
                        gift from the ocean.

6

Green leaves in the wind
Wet earth on my feet
            swallowing raindrops
                        clear from China.

INDIAN SONG: SURVIVAL

1

We went north
            to escape winter
climbing pale cliffs
            we paused   to sleep at the river.

LESLIE MARMON SILKO

2

Cold water   river cold from the north
I sink my body in the shallow
                sink into sand and cold river water.

3

You sleep in the branches of
                pale river willows above me.
I smell you in the silver leaves, mountain lion man
                green willows aren't sweet enough to hide you.

4

I have slept with the river   and
                he is warmer than any man.
At sunrise
        I heard ice on the cattails.

5

Mountain lion, with dark yellow eyes
                you nibble moonflowers
                while we wait.
I don't ask   why do you come
                on this desperation journey north.

6

I am hunted for my feathers
I hide in spider's web
                hanging   in a thin gray tree
                        above the river.
In the night   I hear music
                song of branches   dry leaves scraping the moon.

Voices of the Rainbow

7
Green spotted frogs sing to the river
                    and   I know he is waiting.
Mountain lion shows me the way
              path of mountain wind
              climbing higher
                up
                    up to Cloudy Mountain.

8
It is only a matter of time, Indian
                  you can't sleep with the river forever.
Smell winter and know.

9
I swallow black mountain dirt
        while you catch hummingbirds
           trap them with wildflowers
           pollen and petals
                fallen from the Milky Way.

10
You lie beside me in the sunlight
        warmth around us and
        you ask me if I still smell winter.
Mountain forest wind travels east and I answer:
           taste me,
              I am the wind
           touch me,
              I am the lean gray deer
        running on the edge of the rainbow.

LESLIE   MARMON   SILKO

IN COLD STORM LIGHT

In cold storm light
I watch the sandrock
   canyon rim.

   The wind is wet
      with the smell of piñon.
   The wind is cold
      with the sound of juniper.

         AND THEN
           Out of the thick ice sky
             running   swiftly
             pounding
             swirling above the treetops
          The snow elk come.
          Moving, moving
             white song
               storm wind in the branches.
And when the elk have passed
     behind them
        a crystal trail of snowflakes
        strands of mist
            tangled in rocks
            and leaves.

SUN CHILDREN

   I
Wild ducks
    float with the north wind

They eat dying water spiders
     in fragments of winter light.
Ice shines
       where cattails are yellow
       wind rattles making music.
Ahead of winter
      frozen water
      swirling snow
         They fly
             singing
     South
       south to Sun House
     Here now   we go.

   2
Warm wind   and
      yellow honey flowers returning
Born out of song.
         Water spiders hide in river moss
The ducks come again singing.
      The sun is strong
      His beauty grows inside us
         around us.
      Here now   we come
        early in the morning
        from the east
          at sunrise.
Spring grass
Deer fawn
     sun children.

HAWK AND SNAKE

(*Chinle, June 1972*)

I go back again
      walking slow
away from the houses and stores
and look back once
        or twice
        at the fields and fences
        in the distance.

I began to see the size
          of the sky
           blue beyond all else
          blue, light
            above the pale red earth.
I recall the others here,
  snake coiled on his rocks
  peering out at me from the shade
    hawk   soaring
        silent arcs above the canyon

And then no longer
      blue flower, spiral rock
      spring water.

I am back again
     I sweep high above the hills
     on brown spotted wings
     I peer out from my rocks
       coiled in noontime shade.

THE TIME WE CLIMBED
SNAKE MOUNTAIN

Seeing good places
    for my hands
I grab the warm parts of the cliff
       and I feel the mountain as I climb.
Somewhere   around here
     yellow spotted snake is sleeping   on his rock
       in the sun.

So
  please, I tell them
     watch out,
don't step on the spotted yellow snake
       he lives here.
The mountain is his.

HORSES AT VALLEY STORE

Every day I meet the horses
  With dust and heat they come
     step by step
Pulling the day
  behind them.

At Valley Store
  there is water.
  Gray steel tank
  Narrow concrete trough.

Eyes that smell water,
In a line one by one

> moving with the weight of the sun
> moving through the deep earth heat
They come.

People   with
> water barrels
> in pickups   in wagons
So they pause   and from their distance
> outside of time
They wait.

PREPARATIONS

Dead sheep
> beside the highway.
Belly burst open
> guts and life unwinding on the sand.

The body is carefully attended.
Look at the long black wings
> the shining eyes
Solemn and fat the crows gather
> to make preparations.

> Pull wool from skin
> Pick meat from bone
> tendon from muscle.
Only a few more days
> they say to each other
A few more days and this will be finished.

> Bones, bones
> Let wind polish the bones.
> It is done.

Voices of the Rainbow

Gerald Vizenor

(MINNESOTA CHIPPEWA)

INDIANS AT THE GUTHRIE

limping past the guthrie theater
wounded indian
saluting with the wrong hand

blond children in purple tapestries
building castles
barricades on stage with reservation plans

rehearsing overscream from sand creek
five hundred dead on the mystic river stage

hanging the wrong men
for raising the wrong flags

once more at wounded knee
sniffing glue in gallop
sterno in bemidji
cultural suicides downtown on the reservations

when the theater acts are over
the players mount up for new parties in the hills

TRIBAL STUMPS

tribal mixed bloods
new warriors
every other night
over pale fingers beneath the stairs

flesh tones
feathers retouched like photographs
one generation to the next

old word races
over and over like mission whores

near lake winnibigoshish
stuffed animals
climbing the great red pines

my father returns
with all the mixed bloods

tribal stumps
from the blood-soaked beams of the city

UNHAPPY DIARY DAYS

she returned from the clinic
alone

shadows falling
plum colors of the sun
beneath her eyes

opening and closing closet doors
she told her plants
one by one she was dying

you will be thirty-two
no more

she burned love letters from a felon
counted her shares
her travels
unhappy diary days

she turned her clothes
sleeve by sleeve
across the seasons next year

unhooking the hooks
untying the ties
she undressed for the garden

in the moist september light
she lifted her breasts
hand over hand in flight

with young birds
turning on the wrong trees at dusk
she crashed through the glass

FEBRUARY PARK

for months
my books were stacked

GERALD VIZENOR

33

unswept
like temple stairs

mother wrote
opening the pain at her knees
stiffening words

winter about me again
lamp globes
stained with dead moths

turning against myself
again this year
no fingernails to hide

alone in the parks

watching white women
walking their small dogs like bad dreams

my collar slips off at the curb

february winter
catching dream birds
hearts beating against my hands
burst inside

TROPISMS ON JOHN BERRYMAN

the poet spilled my gin
twice with his hoary party laughter

grazing through the summer chairs
hunchvoiced henry over eighteenth century sighs

graven women under polyester lace
parsing their names to him from the bushes

henry grinning

henry drinking drinking drinking

fathom words
wandering at night from tower hill

kittens wheezing
half a continent on the telephone

pollen tumbling in the nostrils of the saints

his eyes through sparrows
burning holes in picnic poems

henry sitting alone

rows of river mosquitoes
grounded on his sacred blood

lifting his hands to wave
huffy henry
falls in the playground after dark
counting the common strokes of the empty swings

TYRANNY OF MOTHS

tonight the moths
go stitching with their kind
up and down the net

GERALD VIZENOR

they may never know
my light is not my day

they seem so harried
poor peasants in a war

their bodies
would disturb my reading light

my life tonight

switching out the light
we are drawn to another light
farther down the road

THUMBING OLD MAGAZINES

the money men collect in high rise
executive city dumps
bound like old magazines

molding at the center folds
fingernail chips and lip stained
they were not wise enough to turn
hiding one sunday from the next

double wives playing like children
traveling in real hair wigs from the orient
staying alive

and what was your day

nothing new
lawyers in the morning
lunch nineteen stories up with an old foundation

medicine man
previewing promotion plays
all afternoon in the corporate ready room

they praise the little people
assembly lines overseas
running ten-hour production rhythm tapes
enriching the ground floors
without windows

they enlarge the breasts of secretaries
subscribed dumb enough to hold the calls

money wheellock is in conference
planning the next philanthropic overkill

soft white money men
mothered from private schools
with a river view
wash themselves several times a day
washing after play

FAMILY PHOTOGRAPH

among trees
my father was a spruce

corded for tribal pulp
he left the white earth reservation
colonial genealogies
taking up the city at twenty-three

telling stories
sharing dreams from a mason jar

running
low through the stumps at night
was his line

at twenty-three
he waited with the old men
colorless
dressed in their last uniforms
reeling on the nicollet island bridge

arm bands adrift
wooden limbs
men too civilized by war
thrown back to evangelists and charity

no reservation superintendents there
no indian agents
pacing off allotments twenty acres short
only family photographs ashore

no catholics on the wire
tying treaty money to confirmations

in the city
my father was an immigrant
hanging paper flowers
painting ceilings white for a union boss
disguising saint louis park

his weekend women
listened to him measuring my blood at night

downtown rooms were cold
half truths
peeling like blisters of history
two sizes too small

he smiles
holding me in a photograph then
the new spruce
half white
half immigrant
taking up the city and losing at cards

HAIKU   *from* Seventeen Chirps *and* Empty Swings

august heat
even the big green housefly
sits by the fan

october sunflowers
like rows of defeated soldiers
leaning in the frost

mounds of foam
beneath the waterfall
floating silently

fireflies blinking
one alights then disappears
in the dewy grass

upon the pine cones
first flakes of delicate snow
becoming drops of dew

october wind
garage doors open and close
wings of the moth

horse in the frost
like an engine puffing the slopes
missing a breath

autumn sunset
young blue herons step by step
changing the guard

walking the dog
my shadow comes and goes
april moon

beneath the swings
worms meeting after the storm
robins swinging

we are like the leaves
down after a heavy rain
showing our teeth

kennedy is dead
potted window geraniums
waiting to be turned

crack! crack!
his hoe against the garden stones
mother died

in the moonlight
he recognized his old shirt
among the crows

the hail sounded
once or twice a summer
old school bell

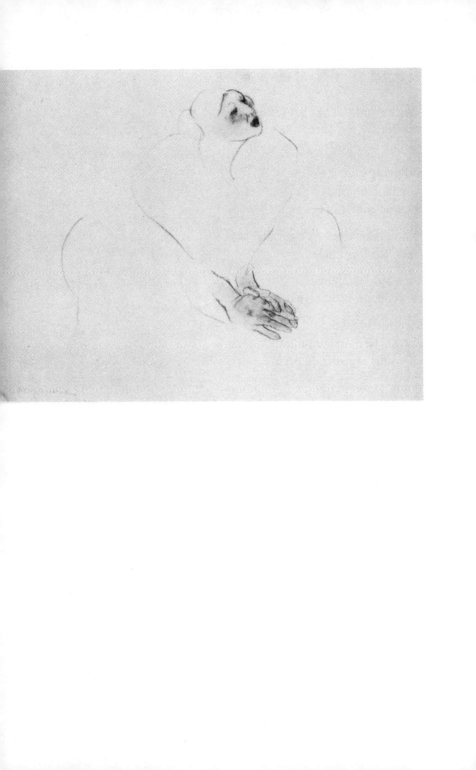

NORTH TO MILWAUKEE

manservants on the last trains
north to milwaukee
hailing mary through the junk

swinging brass keys
low like censers
locking toilets in the depot graves

running between refrigerated cars
stenciled for repairs

between warehouses
sprayed with threats and promises

shadows breaking
across the doors of milk trucks
yawning over the oil grass

dinner under train
death bells ding at every crossing

photographs of the founders
glancing back from the dead water

the phlegm of last rites
stains the sleeves of the survivors

RAISING THE FLAG

without a winter coat
she was two hundred and seventy years
anishinabe time

she learned english
in a cold place for sacred names
milking cows for another race

her brown feet
breaking through her red charity shoes

squaw for the soldiers
who bought her another drink

white city soldiers
cursing her dark eyes

mauling her breasts for the cavalry
without a name

she was down in a civilization she never understood
living forever

when the new soldiers fell
one by one at the bar
she raised in her heart
the sacred flag of the people
dreaming
her children were coming home

SEVEN WOODLAND CROWS

seven woodland crows
stayed all winter
this year
among the white earth trees

down around us on the edge of roads
passing in the eyes of strangers

GERALD VIZENOR

tribal land wire marked
fox runs under rusting plows

stumps for eagles

white winter savages
with brackish blue eyes
snaring their limbs on barbed wire

brackish winter blood

seven woodland crows
stayed all winter
this year
marking the dead
landmen who ran the woodland
out of breath

ANISHINABE GRANDMOTHERS

anishinabe grandmothers
swelling like sweet clover on the dancing fields

stomachs swaying
print dresses smiling on the wind

tribal dream songs
coming from the past without teeth
more beautiful than flowers

dream children touching the earth again
with gnarled fingers

the scars of reservation life
turning under with age

the sacred earth remembers
every flower

grandchildren following
clumsy and clover stained
tasting the rain
singing
the world will change

Janet Campbell Hale

(COEUR D'ALENE)

SALAD LA RAZA

The crisp
Pale green
Lettuce
Caught the sunlight,
Glistened,
As I
Broke the leaves
For my salad,
Lettuce
I'd bought that morning at Safeway,
Remembering how
My family,
For a time,
And off and on,
Lived in dumpy cabin camps,
Moved around,
Picking berries
       beans,

apples,
cherries,
Stripping hops.
I remembered
The dirt,
And sweating
Under a blazing sun
For next to nothing,
And
The babbling,
Laughing
Mexican workers,
Who called themselves "Spanish"
(There were no Chicanos
         in those days)
And looked down
On Indians so much,
"Los Indios" was enough
of a dirty name
In itself.
Eating my crisp and delicious
Safeway salad,
I tried not to think
Of Caesar Chavez.

ON A CATHOLIC CHILDHOOD

Even after Confession,
Sister Mary Leonette told me
(I was six years old at the time)
My soul would be scarred by sin.

This was during catechism.
I had a question:
"Can't you make your guardian angel go away?
Not even while you're going to the toilet?"
Mary Leonette glared at me
And the children laughed.
She was from Vermont and didn't
Like it in grubby old Omak, Washington, all that much.
I thought guardian angels were creepy
And sermons boring,
And when I had to kneel during Mass
I prayed to God
To make it pass quickly
Because my knees ached.
Padre Nostros De En Chalis
Smelling incense
And having to look at a gory
life-size painted statue of
the crucified Christ,
And think of
The poor souls
In purgatory
And a recent sin of my own
I'd never confess:
   I stole my sister's
        plastic glows-in-the-dark Virgin Mary
        And hid it deep within the lilac bush.
God would never understand.

DESMET, IDAHO, MARCH 1969

At my father's wake,
The old people
      Knew me,
    Though I
      Knew them not,
And spoke to me
In our tribe's
Ancient tongue,
Ignoring
The fact
That I
Don't speak
The language,
And so
I listened
As if I understood
What it was all about,
And,
Oh,
How it
Stirred me
To hear again
That strange,
    Softly
     Flowing
Native tongue,
So
Familiar to
My childhood ear.

JANET CAMPBELL HALE

GETTING STARTED

It isn't that I've forgotten
Or don't intend to do
With my life what I
Know I should,
That is, transcend the petty concerns
And live
In truth
And in beauty
according to the
Higher aims of my existence.
Yet,
I have trouble
getting started
somehow
And day by day,
Hour by hour,
Wait,
For the spell
to be broken,
And go on,
Life as usual,
minute by minute,
pulse beat
by
pulse beat,
paying bills,
doing the laundry,
going to work,
putting band-aids
on little scraped knees,
watching TV,

Swept along
    and along.

CINQUE

Can't make excuses for you, Cinque,
You poor son-of-a-bitch,
Can't say,
"Well, he had a rough life, all right,
Very rough, and after all, his heart
was in the right place,
Everything he did being
for The People,"
Because everybody,
Rich, poor, red, black, white, or whatever,
Knew you for what you were,
Fanatic insane killer,
Everybody had your number,
And we all breathed
A collective sigh of relief,
When we found out for certain
That it *was* you
In the big L. A. P. D. shoot-out,
You who went up in a final blaze
Of glory,
Your pitiful charred remains
Found in the L.A. ashes,
When the fire died down.
Cinque, ghetto-product, ex-con
madman who never had a future,
Cinque, you're a legend now.

JANET CAMPBELL HALE

AARON NICHOLAS, ALMOST TEN

He was once a tiny, helpless thing,
A being for whom
I was the very center of the universe,
And even later on,
Watching him as he learned
To walk and talk
And explore the world,
I knew all there was to know
About his sweet, limited life.

Now he has his own thing going,
Quite apart from me,
Interests that do not concern me,
Things I just wouldn't understand,
Secrets shared
With other little boys,
But not with me.

For only a while longer
I'll be able to
Hug his little boy body
And kiss his smooth, soft cheek
And tuck him in at night,
For only a while longer.
I am afraid.

SIX FEET UNDER

Not realizing
That that

Is what
It's all about,
She says, absently,
"I would've
Killed myself
A long time ago . . .
If I wasn't
So afraid,"
And goes
back
To watching *Gunsmoke*
And sipping her
Iced lemonade.

ON DEATH AND LOVE

He lies
Beside me,
Sleeping,
While outside,
    The wind blows,
    Rain falls,
    A dog barks,
We touch, slightly,
Keeping each other
warm. . . .
I stare into the darkness,
Thinking of: Dying,
    Of my aged and infirm mother
    Of my father
    Lying in his

JANET CAMPBELL HALE

                    cold, dark
                    grave,
And I remember,
That I found
My first white hair
That morning.
I turn
to my love,
And snuggle nearer
Until I can feel
his breath.
Still sleeping,
He
Opens his arms
To me.
I lay
My head
Against his chest
And listen
To his heart
beat.

CUSTER LIVES IN HUMBOLT COUNTY

What was it called,
When all that old-time white man trouble
was going on?
All that killing and taking away of home,
of country?
Justifiable genocide or some
such thing, no doubt.

Involuntary manslaughter,
they called it,
When that cop in Humbolt County
Shot the young Pomo last spring,
Shot him and left him
Lying by the roadside,
Hidden in the tall green grass,
Lying bleeding in the spring sunlight,
In the tall green grass,
Involuntary manslaughter,
they called it,
when the Pomo died at last.

All the old, wild-West white man trouble
is over now,
Should be forgotten, they say.
Wild grass grows again at Little Big Horn,
at Steptoe, at Wounded Knee,
Tall grass, swaying in the gentle wind,
covering the old battle scars,
The old healed wounds.
The sun shines warm in a big, clear sky,
All is quiet now,
The past is best forgotten.

JANET CAMPBELL HALE

Lance Henson

(CHEYENNE)

FLOCK

across the road
ice huddles against the trees

there is only a whisper of
leaves among the cottonwoods

and over the joyless valley

snow moves
like an ancient herd

WARRIOR NATION TRILOGY

I

from the mountains we come
lifting our voices for the beautiful
road you have given

we are the buffalo people
we dwell in the light of our father sun
in the shadow of our mother earth

we are the beautiful people
we roam the great plains without fear
in our days the land has taught us oneness
we alone breathe with the rivers
we alone hear the song of the stones

2

oh ghost that follows me
find in me strength to know the wisdom
of this life

take me to the mountain of my grandfather
i have heard him all night
singing among the summer leaves

3
great spirit

make me whole
i have come this day with my spirit
i am not afraid
for i have seen in vision
the white buffalo
grazing the frozen field
which grows near the full circle
of this
world

LANCE HENSON

AMONG HAWKS

we have watched again
   our own guilt disguised
      stalking the sullen wind

carrying our own words the crows
  in the worn sky wait remembering
                too late

the reasons
  for our being
     among them

TRAVELS WITH THE BAND-AID ARMY

strangers on a train
following their patterns
old friends
sitting on bus stop benches
soft breathing whispers
across a battered field
filled with worn tires
laid to rest

old man alone rocking in a chair at twilight

flat voices in the choirbox
              numbered faces

limp throatless words
  dancing in shadows of snow

SUNDOWN AT DARLINGTON 1878

the children enter
to sit near the fire

we have come a long way
to this place
where the sun through gray
winter skies whispers our
names

dreams fill the sleep of the old
their voices touch the darkness
making it holy

we have come a long way

the colors of winter weigh heavy
on this worn country

there is no sound from the trees
yet at night the ghost still dances
among the horses
the dogs still
wander the river land
barking on and on
into the damp
fall wind

OLD MAN TOLD ME

it is enough for me
the crows of winter calling for rain

LANCE HENSON

enough that the children still hear me
in their fires

yet beyond
the wars still crush the fragile hills

it is enough
still

when smoking
i must
weep

WOOD FLOOR DREAMS

1

i have come upon the visage again
  of crows at four flying across the
    winter moon

of wolves watching shadows on the flowing dark

of faces brushing the older trees

2

i sit near the vacuum of sleep

i run with my kin to the snow forest where
    words rest as from a long journey

3

somewhere turning in the river
    of winter

                    these few
                              with their lives
sing in the rush
        of water over smooth stones
                                    leaving their names
on our mantles
        at waking

M O T H

what falls before us like snow
                does not remember its own

                        light returns from a long
journey without its brother pain

for no reason upon waking we find
                our questions

hanging from the
                        old
                            sky

S L E E P   W A T C H

you enter the areas beyond veiled light
        there is in your attitude a calling of entities

the heavy darkness bears up
        giving you a boundless void
                and at once

oblivious to summer and the moving
webs
    you
        drift toward the child
         within you sleeping

SCATTERED LEAVES

rain on the far tip of the grove
    shade near the waiting trees
        there is hint of winter
             be calmed

it is not ingratitude sitting near you
though the worn bells of the child lamb
tremble

we come upon beginnings
   moths fly deep into their own
      fading lees
         it is like this every
place

names
on empty cups
filling all wind
      fall
      day

BETWEEN RIVERS AND SEAS

in the visions of sailors
   there are no sweeter moments
      than dawn paling the windless sea

when frost on iron railings reflects the
  forgetful sky

when ships of shepherds come at noon
   bringing in their hands first signs of rain

when on and on
   the song of the child
      rings in the heart
              of ancient men

CURTAIN

it was cold then in the cautious hours
before first light
            beside my brothers
my sister
      wrapped
         in webbed sleep
               it
was colder
then than it can ever be

though the eyes of the dead at times
reflect the same rising wings

Voices of the Rainbow

                    the
                          same
first
       dust

COMANCHE GHOST DANCE   *an impression*

we will return to life
we will stay in the sun long before the shadows are borne

there will be no distance between our words and the
banished moon

in all that grows while the winter reaps
we will live again

WE ARE A PEOPLE

days pass easy over these ancient hills

i walk near a moccasin path overgrown with
rusted cans and weeds
i stand in the forest at sunset waiting for
a prayer from the rising wind

it is this way forever in this place
there is no distance between the name of my
race and the owl calling
nor the badger's gentle
plodding

LANCE HENSON

we are a people born under symbols
that rise from the dust to touch us
that pass through the cedars where
our old ones sleep
                    to tell us of their dreams

OTHER

before dawn i rose thirsty
and cold

watching the east i knew
there were other moments
everywhere

thirsty without me

RAIN

small bird
tracks

on a damp
stone

   melt

CRAZY HORSE

dawn

rose like a hand at the edge of dark

in the transparent mist the warrior
stood as if
listening
to a
bell

in
the
hollow
wind

EPITAPH: SNAKE RIVER

again the light of
the silver stream
glistens the taste
of iron the blood
of the young arrives
oh lute of the prairie
wind we have listened
too long the light
of our shining bones
betrays us our last
colorless dreams are
fallen

LANCE HENSON

67

where are we come that
we must stand this
alone

BAY POEM

where from the watch towers
the rust of
shipwrecks
shine

bar
where the sailor
remembered
peace and
laughed

epitaph soaked
          sponges
across bars

endless
          damp
streets

lovely moonshine
at

              2
          a m

on the edge
of
rain

SITTING ALONE IN TULSA
THREE A.M.

round dance of day has gone

a siren's scream splashes the blinds like ice
a fly sits frozen on a yellow plastic cup
the end tables huddle in pairs

sale at renbergs on ladies shoes
    felt squares and soft knits at the mill outlet

whatever i have done today has gone without me

the edges of the city and the pale moon reflect
    in the same river

how easily we forget

IMAGE OF CITY

white dusk moved ahead of them
    farther than time

the worn clicks of their shoes
    left pale rooms

light snow in the streets answered those
    cries of blind trembling flowers

in the sacred morning
    the cheap hotels stood in shadows of
        each
        with
        a practiced
            solemnity

LANCE HENSON

OLD STORY

he will have turned
the last corridors
by now he will have
stood weeping in the
sad museum where
wrinkled hands hang
tired from praying

by now even the dust
on his shoulders will
have forsaken him and
at last he will turn
facing you

but you will not
recognize him
though his tears
cloud your eyes
with
      pain

ANNIVERSARY POEM FOR THE
CHEYENNES WHO FELL AT SAND CREEK

when we have come this long way
past cold gray fields
past the stone markers etched with the
names they left us

we will speak for the first time to the season
to the ponds

touching the dead grass

our voices the color of watching

POEM FOR CARROLL
DESCENDANT OF CHIEFS

again the call of the winter birds

among the domino men
   in a must-filled room
      there is talk of thieves

in a broken house the risingbears
   watch the old man roll a cigarette

shadows of his smoke curl yellow against
   the ragged paper curtain

while the bone moon
   watches from a windless sky

Anna Walters

(PAWNEE / OTO)

MY BROTHERS . . .

My brothers, for many winters now
  you've been triumphant with your game.
Your rules were made with words
  my tongue found hard to know.
This wide mouth of mine no longer
  remembers the smiles of not so long ago.
But my eyes remember, my brothers,
  the time you won my chief's blanket,
  his most prized possession.
You walked away tall,
  haughtily wrapped in an old one's scarlet robe.
The blanket didn't fit you,
  although many times you wore it.
It was meant for only one!
Your pale skin you left uncovered
  shone too brightly competing with "Old Man,"
  the Sun.
My chief had known much hunger,

loneliness he'd met long ago.
Old Age was his companion,
  Dignity held his hand.
His blanket was his last possession.
But once again you played your petty game
  and once again, you won.
I have thought of my chief many times.
Still I see his long gray hair
  hugging the sides of his head.
My eyes remember the pain he suffered
  when you stripped him of his pride.
He wore that well, my friend.
My heart remembers the sorrow,
  the wound is fresh.
So I have watched you, my brothers,
  each time you've played your game.
My mind is storing away all that my eyes see
  and my ears hear.
I must be learning your ways well,
  for my tongue is cruel and quick to move.
The taste is bitter in my mouth.
Now you guard me suspiciously wondering why
  I spit at your feet while smiling into your eyes.
You wonder at my excuses for not playing your many games
  and yet—you worry when I do.
Are you afraid of the tactics I use, my friend?
Remember, I learned them from you.
The rules are not yet clear in my mind,
  you change them daily at sunrise.
Your memory, unlike mine, is short.
  —My brothers, pity me,
      I am ashamed
      for soon I will be as you. . . .

A TEACHER TAUGHT ME

1

a teacher taught me
more than she knew
patting me on the head
putting words in my hand
—"pretty little *Indian* girl"
saving them—
going to give them
back to her one day . . .
show them around too
cousins and friends
laugh and say—"aye"

2

binding by sincerity
hating that kindness
eight years' worth
third graders heard her
putting words in my hand
—"we should bow our heads
in shame for what we did
to the American Indian"
saving them—
going to give them
back to her one day . . .
show them around too
cousins and friends
laugh and say—"aye"

3

in jr. hi
a boy no color
transparent skin
except sprinkled freckles
followed me around
putting words in my hand
—"squaw, squaw, squaw"
(not that it mattered,

hell, man, I didn't know
what squaw meant . . .)
saving them—
going to give them
back to him one day . . .
show them around too
cousins and friends
laugh and say—"aye"

4

slapping open handed
transparent boy
across freckled face
knocking glasses down
he finally sees
recollect a red
handprint over minutes
faded from others
he wears it still
putting words in my hand
—"sorry, so sorry"
saving them—
going to give them
back to him one day
show them around too
cousins and friends
laugh and say—"aye"

I AM OF THE EARTH

I am of the earth
She is my mother
She bore me with pride
She reared me with love
She cradled me each evening
She pushed the wind to make it sing
She built me a house of harmonious colors
She fed me the fruits of her fields

ANNA WALTERS

She rewarded me with memories of her smiles
She punished me with the passing of time
And at last, when I long to leave
She will embrace me for eternity

SIMPLICITY AIMS CIRCULARLY

Simplicity aims circularly.
Directly removing, discreetly returning
Elusively life's mystery.

HARTICO

Grandpa, I saw you die in the Indian hospital at Pawnee,
   twenty years ago, but look who is talking, you know
   of it all too well. . . .

   I can measure time. You, yourself, showed me how.
   But how does one count another man's loss? Do I count
   on my fingers the memories and think of the stars as
   my tears?

Grandpa, beautiful brown old Oto!
   At Red Rock, do you still cross the creek to walk
   your rolling green hills? Has time, with her sense
   of duty, covered your tracks with mine?

   Then let me climb the hills for you.
   My children shall follow me with theirs after them.
   One day, we will be so many that we could hold hands,
   form a circle and dance around the earth.

Grandpa, to you, I close my eyes from distractions
and open my heart. . . .

Remember when I was a rabbit?
It was the manner of a child who knew nothing but play.
You could not be but what you were. A handsome, but tired,
powerful old bear.

I saw you and know this to be true. You would pull yourself
upright and scan my horizon. Hands up as though you would
advise me some caution. In the early morning sun, I saw it
circle you with its brilliance. It seemed to me to be a
sign. Then down you relaxed, signaling me with your
spirit. Rabbit, be happy! Go with the morning!

Grandpa, I saw an old bear hold a rabbit
ever so gently in one huge hand. I heard him sing bear words
rabbit did not know but could understand.

The bear was sleepy. The rabbit could tell because the
bear would often yawn. . . .

Grandpa, the bear would then speak. This is what he said.
"Rabbits are fond of songs that sing about frybread!"

Old bear gave the song to the rabbit. They held it
between them to make it strong with laughter from
the rabbit and the bear.

There is not another one like it. My children have
searched for one. I brought the song here now
so you can look at it. We will sing it.

Grandpa, old bear has passed away but the rabbit remains.
For four nights, old bear lay alone, very cold
silently greeting people who came to warm him with their words.
All for you, they drummed and sang in Oto. It was to tell

ANNA WALTERS

77

the people of the world it would be wise to mourn as we were
one less, and therefore not so strong.

On the fourth day, old bear left the rabbit far behind.
He began a lonesome journey, for which he was in no hurry,
but the next in line.

All the people gathered to bring old bear tears that pale day.
It made a simple rabbit very proud when you gracefully
accepted them, in the old way. . . .

Grandpa, I see the rabbit, now and then, in a water mirror.
He comes and goes. Years have shaped a bear around a jumpy
rabbit. The bear sings. I know it. Within himself,
he sings of rabbits and frybread.

Grandpa, I tell you this. It comes from memories of long ago.
It was something that you said.

Carter Revard

(OSAGE)

THE COYOTE

There was a little rill of water, near the den,
That showed a trickle, all the dry summer
When I was born. One night in late August it rained;
The thunder waked us. Drops came crashing down
In dust, on stiff blackjack leaves, on lichened rocks,
Rain came in a pelting rush down over the hill,
Wind puffed wet into the cave; I heard sounds
Of leaf-drip, rustle of soggy branches in gusts of wind.

And then the rill's tune changed: I heard a rock drop
And set new ripples gurgling in a lower key.
Where the new ripples were, I drank, next morning,
Fresh muddy water that set my teeth on edge.
I thought how delicate that rock's poise was:
The storm made music, when it changed my world.

DRIVING IN OKLAHOMA

On humming rubber along this white concrete
    lighthearted between the gravities
of source and destination like a man
      halfway to the moon
    in this bubble of tuneless whistling
at seventy miles an hour from the windvents,
      over prairie swells rising
    and falling, over the quick offramp
that drops to its underpass and the truck
      thundering beneath as I cross
with the country music twanging out my windows,
      I'm grooving down this highway feeling
technology is freedom's other name when
                      —a meadowlark
    comes sailing across my windshield
      with breast shining yellow
      and five notes pierce
        the windroar like a flash
      of nectar on mind
gone as the country music swells up and
    drops me wheeling down
    my notch of cement-bottomed sky
    between home and away
               and wanting
to move again through country that a bird
   has defined wholly with song
      and maybe next time see how
he flies so easy, when he sings.

GETTING ACROSS

Hanging
　　　　out under the bridge
　　by fingertips and a toe
　　　　　between ledge and girder, high
　　over deep water and thinking,
　　　　　　I can't swim,
　　　　unreachable by the older boys
　　　　　　who've made it across, he watches
　　the steel-blue flash of wings
　　　　　and chestnut bellies of barnswallows
shooting and swirling around him,
　　　　　　　　　below him,
　　　a two-foot gar's black shadow
　　　　　　in the green-brown water beneath,
and before he weakens has
　　　let the toe slip gently and
　　　　swung down
　　　like a pendulum, hand
　　over hand along the girder to
　　　　　　where the others perch
　　　　　　　　on the concrete ledge,
　has kicked up his right leg onto the ledge and
　　　　　been pulled to its safety,
　can look back now at the swallow's easy
　　　　curve upward,
　　　　　　　its flutter and settling
　　　gently into the cup
　of feather-lined mud there nestling
　　on the shining girder's side
　　where he has passed his death.

NOT JUST YET

This burly son of a bitch,
      when we got outside the beerjoint
he moved between me and the light
        and loomed up close and said,
    "Think you can whip me, do you?"
I couldn't see well, facing the bright light.
      "She don't want to dance with you," I said.
He reached his hand out, laid it on my shoulder,
      and pulled the other fist back.
    "My brother's got a tire-tool, over there," I said.
He took a step back, looked sideways
        and saw Jim holding the tire-iron
    there by our car and watching us.
      "Grady," he said, loud over his shoulder,
        "I want a little help, here."
A gray-haired drunk with glasses
    climbed out of his Ford's front seat
        and a sagging blonde came with him.
    He was holding the snub-nosed pistol
loose in his right hand.
      "You just go right ahead, Billy Don," he said,
      "Betty and me can dance when you're finished.
        There won't nobody interrupt you any."
That was when headlights came around the curve
      and shone in my face.
"Here comes that god damn state patrolman, Grady.
    Better put the gun up," Billy Don said.
Before the black-and-white car had pulled up and parked
    they'd gone inside
        and had the juke-box playing
    the "Long Gone Lonesome Blues"

Voices of the Rainbow

and Billy Don was dancing
　　　　half buried in the sagging blonde
　　when the state patrolman went in.

NORTH OF SANTA MONICA

1

It's midnight in a drizzling fog
　　　　on Sunset Avenue and we are walking
　　through the scent of orange blossoms and past
　a white camellia blown down or flung by someone
　　onto rainblack asphalt waiting
for the gray Mercedes sedan to run over
　　　　and smash its petals and leave us walking in
　the smell of Diesel exhaust with
　　　　　　orange-blossom bouquet.

2

Where the next blue morning
　　　　and the gray Pacific meet
　　as the Palisades fall away
　　　　two sparrowhawks are beating
　their tapered wings in place
　　　　　　till a jay or chewink stray too far
from its thorny scrub to get back,
　　　　and the female suddenly towers,
half-closes her wings and stoops
　　　　like a dagger falling,
but down the steep slope rockets past them and turns
　again into updraft to the clifftops and hovers
　　　　as the jay peers out through thorns
　and the lines of white surf come in.

ANOTHER SUNDAY MORNING

What I walked down to the highway
through the summer dawn for
was the Sunday funnies,
or so I thought,
but what I remember reading there
in the shadowless light
among meadowlarks singing
was tracks in the deep warm dust
of the lane where it parted
with its beige dryness the meadow's dew:
the sleek trail where a snake had crossed
and slid into tall grass;
the stippled parallels
with marks between them where
a black blister-beetle had dragged
its bulbous belly across
in search of weeds more green;
the labyrinth of lacelike
dimples left by a speed-freak
tiger-beetle's sprints that ended
where it took wing
with a little blur of dust-grains;
and stepping through the beetle-trails
the wedge-heels and sharp-clawed hands of a skunk-track
crossing unhurried and walking
along the ditch to find
an easy place for climbing;
not far past that,
a line of cat-prints running
straight down the lane and ending
with deep marks where it leaped

across the ditch to the meadow
                for birds asleep or wandering baby rabbits:
        and freshly placed this morning
                        the slender runes
            of bob-whites running, scuffles
                                    of dustbaths taken,
                and there ahead
        crouched low at the lane-edge
                        under purple pokeweed-berries
four quail had seen me,
                and when I walked slowly
                    on toward them, instead
                        of flying they ran
                            with a fluid scuttling
                    on down the lane and stopped frozen
                            till I came too close
            then quietly when
            I expected an explosion
                    of wings they took off low and whispering
and sailed, rocking and tilting,
                    out over the meadow's tall bluestem,
                                dropped down and were gone until
I heard them whistling, down by the little pond,
            and whistled back so sharply
                        that when I got back to the house
                                they still were answering
                and one flew into the elm
            and whistled from its shadows
                        up over the porch where I sat
        reading the funnies while the kittens
                played with the headlines
                            till when the first gold sunlight
        tipped the elm's leaves he flew

CARTER REVARD

                    back out to the meadow and sank
                              down into sun-brilliant dew
                                        on curving wings,
              and my brothers and sisters waked
                         by the whistling came pouring out
        onto the porch and claimed their share
                                   of the Sunday funnies,
              and I went on to read
                         the headlines of World War Two
        with maps of the struggling armies leaving
              tank-tracks over the dunes of Libya
                         and the navies churning their wakes
              of phosphorescence in the Coral Sea
        where the ships went down on fire
                   and the waves bobbed and flamed
        with the maimed survivors screaming
        in Japanese or English until
their gasoline-blistered heads
              sank down to the tiger-sharks
        and the war was lost or won
                         for children sitting in sunlight
        believing their cause was just
                   and knowing it would prevail
                         as the dew vanished away.

E S P

I know that mind
                    is only matter—
        but will someone please explain
                         what matter is?

In 1895, for instance, Roentgen
        quite accidentally saw that a screen
    was fluorescing when his cathode-ray
            machine was on;
        discovered X-rays thus, and so
    the concept *matter* had to be revised—
and still more radically when, next year,
            Becquerel found his halides fogged
                    by some invisible emanation
        out of uranium ore, not sent by man.
The problem is that down in 1972
        I've got no phosphor screens,
    no silver halides,
            to let me know of such great accidents
        when things from outer space sweep through this mind:
                    of course,
            these wrinkles on the face tell something,
    and language helps, its metaphors transpose
        invisible joy to visible love—see,
            like stones in ultraviolet darkness,
    faces of lovers luminesce,
                their black silver smiles
                    curving like Saturn's rings—
        but most cloud-chambers of language
        are obsolete, they catch
                only what's looked for;
            the unimagined nectar goes through
                    and the tongue spits coffee-grounds.
But lately I have thought of just
                the right sensitive receiver:
        it is a wilderness big enough
        to find a vision in
            while quite alone.

CARTER REVARD

So yesterday I made my lot
      by not raking the lawn
           and watching a two-year-old run
                  through falling leaves;
        and sure enough the message came when
                      he fell with them
            and then got up
and caught one in the air,
               a mulberry leaf that time
      had turned bright yellow,
           with static-spots of rust.
I'll look tomorrow at how the birds fly dark
        against the snow,
      and how snowflakes come sailing into focus
              against my windshield,
        and in the mirror how my beard turns white.
And maybe later
      when my SELF has cooled
                near absolute zero
      it will grow super-conductive
    like a helium-crystal laser, impossible but
               so sensitive
that touched by the *gegenschein* it would
            flash out a Lazarus-light
   on memory's moiré,
      and there would float into view
         the hologram of all my scattered days,
their storms contained as a brilliant play of things
      that meadows could understand as rain,
         and stars as a zodiac of lightnings.
But maybe light is not the place to look:
    I know that as my deafness grows
        to sounds that come through air,

vibrations through these bones
come in always louder;
and it may be my skull
is all the hope I have
to place against the vibrant spheres
and hear them singing—
I used to put my head
against a telephone pole
and hear the wires humming
down through the pole, never needing
to tap their tightstrung copper to be in
on what was said across those miles
of empty blowing prairie
on the coldest winter day.

ADVICE FROM EUTERPE

They hire you for the silk to line their budgets
and give you immortal tenure
among their well-thumbed leaves
until you spin;
but you must never come out
of that cocoon: your life's the single thread
spun for their satiny profit.
So, if they should discover
that you're no spinner and have been chewing
apart on your *Asclepias* leaves,
you'd better split that instant,
shake out your wings on the wind and rise
like a Monarch to the pungence waiting
in mountain meadows

Voices of the Rainbow

where snow-water leaps—
on wings too bright and bitter
for the hookbilled shrike to swallow.

COMING OF AGE IN THE COUNTY JAIL

—I see they worked you over. What you in for?
—Oh, I took this kiddie-car out of a guy's back yard, Friday
                                        midnight.
—What in the world gave you the idea for that?
—Celebrate my birthday. Me and George decided we'd haul it up
        on top the Mound, ride down on that kiddie-car,
        see if we could finish off the wine on the way down.
—That how you got the black eye and stitches, no doubt.
—Not hardly. Turned out the guy whose yard we took it from
        was a city cop, he saw us put it in our car
        and start off down the Mound Road.
—Where'd they catch up with you?
—We got out near the Mound and here came three patrol cars
                                        with sirens
        and red lights flashing, blocked off the road,
        big mob of police jumped out with guns.
—How did the dialogue go after that?
—Mostly we said "ow" and "that's enough." I made the mistake
        of hitting back at a couple. After they got me down
        in back of the car with handcuffs on behind my back,
        they beat me on the shoulder blades with blackjacks.
        This cut in my eyebrow's from a pistol, though.
—Yeah, looks like it. What are you charged with now?
—There's a pretty good list of things they mentioned. Felony,
        for taking the kiddie-car, which the officer valued

at over fifty dollars; then there's assaulting an officer,
resisting arrest, driving with open bottle,
disturbing the peace, so on and so on.
—Well, nobody wants to have his kid's things stolen, especially
police.
But maybe that lawyer can get the charge reduced
to misdemeanor, once things cool down a little.
They told me fifteen minutes was all I had,
I'll start back now. Well, don't wander off.
—No, I kind of think they'll let me stay till the hearing. Besides,
the service here's just great, and gourmet cooking.
Well, here's the man. Thanks for dropping in.

ON THE BRIGHT SIDE

When the green grass rose in the spring
our Jersey's milk turned yellow
with cream and tasted musky
with different weed-flavors; and she'd
be bellowing to be milked
before the sun got up—which was all right,
it gave us longer days, especially weekends.
One disadvantage though
of getting up so early
was that we'd generally watch the sun come up,
and mornings when it was red and slow
we'd make a game of staring at its rising
until our eyes were filled with slow
blood-bubbles and
gold balloons floating
transparently over meadows with

birds winging darkly through them—
this blinded us of course
                    to other things,
        so when we went to breakfast
inside the flyspecked house the air was dim
                as a cathedral, with white glasses
                    of milk standing calmly
                            for hands to reach and bring
        their creamy coldness up
    to dazzled eyes and mouth,
            and the chunk of butter melting
        into the bowl of hot oatmeal
            swam out of focus like
    a tiny sun as we poured
flurries of sugar-crystals down from spoons upon it
        and stirred in Jersey cream, then
                crumbled the toast-with-butter in it
and spooned up crunch-chewy pieces
                            like morning sunlight
        while the roaches went scrambling for crumbs
    on threadbare oilcloth and our fledgling
                wild goldfinch chirruped, waiting
for the fattened roaches we'd bring him on pins as soon
        as the sun got out of our eyes
                and into our hungry bellies.

"BUT STILL IN ISRAEL'S PATHS THEY SHINE"

Six hundred dark feet the cliffs
            from the crash of Atlantic swells

CARTER REVARD

93

beetle up over their surf
and its patches of seaweed tangling
the waves' drive shoreward
pulsed by the miles off gray
of storms
to this sunlit scene,
us seated on green headland
with slow-grazing sheep dotted whitely along
gentle slopes to the lighthouse
looking across that wave-thrash at blurred
rock-bands and strata holding
a million years of sleet and blossoms crushed
to a band of brown;
us thinking how
down on that shingle walking
we saw this morning the million
pebbles brought down from the cliffs' monochrome to lie
all streaked and dappled, spotted and milky and veined,
not one like another but all
rounded and smoothly
rubbing together in wetness; us
remembering how
down in the tidal pool's depths by the boulders
a powder-blue jellyfish was pulsing
upward and downward in that bluegreen clearness
as fragile as joy in time
yet riding the Atlantic's power;
us climbing down at noontime all
the way to the stream's mouth where
its last waterfall pours whitely down
to the cove and its peppersalt beach;
us seeing in noonlight how tiny crab-spiders sidle upon
sand-brilliants and

its grains rough-shaped on palms
as the cliffs where seabirds
soar and dive,
grains crowding like white
faces in terminal lobbies eroded
by grief and joy, pouring
from the hand like pieces
of broken planets tumbling and
flashing
in space;
us saying: the revolution we work for
is revelation and the eyes to see
these shining things and how
they change, and pass,
and are the same.

HOME MOVIES

The elms have to fight
a disease that's withered all
except a few still green by ponds
way out on stony prairie
and some here in the yard
by the smooth concrete foundations
of the torn-down motorhouse
which their roots are slowly breaking;
they survived my grandfather
who chopped them down each year
and now they bristle tall with shade
for my mother, nearing his age—
just one that stood next to the house

I grew up in, survived its passing
        away in orange flame one night,
    and stands half charred
  half withered in the pale March light
        with buds just greening on the west and two
bluebirds flitting querulous about to judge
        if its loose bark has hollows
    strong enough for their nest—
it probably won't, and I don't know
  whether this roll of Super-8 I've taken
    will even show the bluebirds there
in that pale sky and dying, greening tree;
  so, since my mother won't get into the picture,
    I'll shoot the last part now on all
her running, jumping, climbing grandchildren
        stomp-dancing out there on the lawn
    where the living room used to be.

JANUARY 15 AS A NATIONAL HOLIDAY

The Sixties, I think, were not a total loss:
Things got a little better for blacks and Indians,
Standing Bear's kids, or Martin Luther King's—
Only the money's color counts, in Caesar's Palace. . . .

At Tahoe, we floated out over light blue transparence
And saw below us the wave-lights dancing on firm sand,
Or we splashed ashore and lay on the hot heavy sand
To look up at cool mountains and cool blue sky.

As we walked out a cluster of children, ooing
Round a marshy place, parted and let us look down

At a frog being swallowed by a garter-snake, hind legs first,
The frog occasionally croaking as though in despair.

When we left the Sierras behind, eastward from Tahoe,
We came twisting down and down and out into dryness
And southward along the Carson Valley the tires went whining
As the motor fluttered under the airconditioner's wheeze

And trees shrank down into thorny weeds and cactus
That dwindled away as the soil spilled off in the wind
Leaving rocks and ashcrust, we moved between rough upthrusts
Of sandstone and basalt; then off to our left we saw

A slash of rock-choked gully start and go twisting
Where through those dry pebbles some alkaline spring
Oozed its liquid around gray willow roots
And the scar zigzagged greener, grew a dustgreen snake

That slid down into burning green alfalfa depths
In a cobalt sky among lines of Lombardy poplars
And brown bales clustered across jadegreen lushness
As we slowed our speed, turned from the shimmering highway

On a street between houses, grocerystore, gaspumps, movie,
A Legion Hall; and saw, driving past, their indoor swimming pool
Like the desert's heart where it quivered bluegreen with chlorine—
. . . We hit one slot, in Las Vegas, for fifty cents.

SUPPORT YOUR LOCAL POLICE DOG

The night before my Uncle Carter got shot
Trying to hijack a load of bootleg whiskey,
He dressed fit to kill, put on his lilac hairoil,
And leaned down to the mirror in our living room

CARTER REVARD

97

To comb the hair back over his bald spot, humming
"Corinne, Corinne, where have you been so long?"
I don't know if "Corinne" tipped the other bunch off,
But I hope he put it to her before they killed him.
I bet if there was any he was getting his.
—Jesus, I never saw him standing still
Or lying down, till they led me past his coffin.
He should have been born a lord in Boswell's time,
Though he'd most likely been laid up with gout
Before he was forty, had that kind of drive.
More drive than brains though. Hell, man out on parole
For robbing a bank, and his hip not very long healed
Where the cop in ambush shot him trying to surrender,
Had no more sense than go after those bottled-in-bonders
From Kansas City. You KNOW they'd be in cahoots
With all the local crooks and laws. We couldn't
See why he'd let himself get talked into trying.
My Uncle Dwain said it was a put-up job,
Carter knew too much, the gang had him bumped off.

Well, the last time I was home for a visit,
Leaving behind these earnest city people
Who keep DISCOVERING crime and poverty
Like tin cans tied to their suburbs' purebred tails
Till they run frothing, yapping for law and order,
I thought of the big police dog Carter brought home
His last time there and kenneled by the chickenhouse:
Nobody was going to steal OUR stock, by God.
(Later the damn dog got to killing turkeys
On a neighbor's place; we had to let it be shot.)
—The gilt mirror he'd gazed at his bald spot in
Had been demoted, now hung dim in the bathroom.
I patted my Old Spice lather on and shaved
As suavely as he had combed, and smelled as good.

He never lived to grow white whiskers like mine;
I knew the smartest crooks don't ever need guns,
And I would never walk out into the night
To get myself shot down, the way he did.
I've got more brains. But while he lived, I admit,
He was my favorite uncle; guts, charm, and drive.
He would have made a perfect suburban mayor—
Or maybe, manager for some liquor chain.

DISCOVERY OF THE NEW WORLD

The creatures that we met this morning
marveled at our green skins
and scarlet eyes.
They lack antennae
and can't be made to grasp
your proclamation that they are
our lawful food and prey and slaves,
nor can they seem to learn
their body-space is needed to materialize
our oxygen absorbers—
which they conceive are breathing
and thinking creatures whom they implore
at first as angels or (later) as devils
when they are being snuffed out
by an absorber swelling
into their space.
Their history bled from one this morning
while we were tasting his brain
in holographic rainbows
which we assembled into quite an interesting

                    set of legends—
                         that's all it came to, though
               the colors were quite lovely before we
               poured them into our time;
                    the blue shift bleached away
       meaningless circumstance and they would not fit
       any of our truth-matrices—
                    there was, however,
         a curious visual echo in their history
                 of our own coming to their earth;
  a certain General Sherman
                  had said concerning a group of them
                       exactly what we were saying to you
                 about these creatures:
           it is our destiny to asterize this planet,
             and they will not be asterized,
                    so they must be wiped out.
  We need their space and oxygen
             which they do not know how to use,
                       yet they will not give up their gas unforced,
       and we feel sure,
              whatever our "agreements" made this morning,
                    we'll have to kill them all:
                       the more we cook this orbit,
              the fewer next time round.
  We've finished burning all their crops
                 and killed their cattle.
                They'll have to come into our pens
             and then we'll get to study
  the way our heart attacks and cancers spread among them,
              since they seem not immune to these.
       If we didn't have this mission it might be sad
              to see such helpless creatures die,

but never fear,
the riches of this place are ours
and worth whatever pain others may have to feel.
We'll soon have it cleared
as in fact it is already, at the poles.
Then we will be safe, and rich, and happy here forever.

Thomas Peacock

(ANISHINABE)

IN RESPECT OF THE ELDERLY

Let your eyes look at old people
    and be lonely
wind spirits sailing death songs
birch trees sing to me in winter
brother owl has told me
respect your elders

FEAR

Stuffed owls drum in my heart
when I am afraid
meet me when loons cry
we shall share our courage

EARTH SONG

It is not the earth that I worship
but what is behind it
my feathers speak Chippewa
our invisible tongues of silence
understand

FOR THE CHILDREN

Anishinabe children sing songs of sleep
when grandfather tells wa-na-bo-zho stories
and dream visions of playing with lightning
from a perch high up in the clouds
Anishinabe children sing songs of sleep
and dream visions of wa-na-bo-zho
thanking the Great One

ANDONIS, MY DAUGHTER

Andonis is the spring song like
sun spirits are manito's together
maple sugar in its first taste, me-na-wah
samaras on rainy days blossom
pierce the sky in three lifetimes
air winy with rain
red rim on evenfall
Andonis is the spring song, me-na-wah—

SIX EAGLES

Red on sun sky sail
their feathers
six eagles over Hinckley
someone has died
I think of Ba-ka-a-quay, my son
who awoke the morning last
and told me visions of thunderbirds
Will twenty eagles pay homage to him?

Anita Endrezze-Probst

(YAQUI)

RAVEN / MOON   *adapted from a Northwest Coast legend*
                                    For Barbara Endrezze

I

In First People's sky there is no Moon.
The shaman stirs the vigil fires;
vague nights confuse the spirit's travels.

The smell of seaweed, pickled
red and brown in its own dark brine,
awakens the napping girl,
her fingers lazily burrowing
into heavy warm loam.
Behind her, the pressing black pines;
In her hair, the tangle
of thin, damp briers.

The island's trees and shrubs
hug tight the coastal rocks.
At her feet, small silver-backed fish
dance like crescents in the foam.

Loosened berries fall
into pools of waterstones,
hidden among tidal searoots
like red fish eggs.
She is the fisherman's daughter,
the keeper of Moon and its light.
She is the Woman with Medicine Eyes;
Her name means Stranger.

Medicine stones speak
in smooth wind-rounded words.
They rub like sandstone
against her palms. Raven's eyes
lock tight in her skull.
His magic is quiet, sly.
From among the berry thicket,
a spiraling leaf blesses her tongue.
Nestled in her womb, it grows.
When the child is born,
his nose is beaked.

2

Medicine stones roll like lost heads.
Silently, the shaman studies each sign:
Tides bend toward the woman's lodge,
Earth Children tremble, birds fly in circles.

Inside the braided basket,
the box is still.
Box within a box within a box
each painted, inlaid with pearled
abalone shell and whalebone.
Lifting the Moon netting,

the woman shakes out fringes
of deer hooves and puffin beaks.
She tosses the Moon
to her wild-eyed son.
He balances the milky sphere
between crooked lips.
The Moon is a plaything
in the hands of a child.

When he cries, pointing
to the boarded smoke hole,
she opens it. Like black water,
Night falls into her hands
spilling into the corners
of her lodge. Her son sings,
pulling feathers from under his skin,
shaking out wings, blue-black, strong.
With Moon in his bill, Raven flies out,
flinging it past his curving wings,
far up into the sky.

Moon settles slowly, an embryo
in Night Maiden's belly.
In the village, the fisherman's daughter
buries the empty Moon boxes
deep inside her.
At their birth, she dies.
Set adrift in cold waters,
under a blanket of Red Moons,
her body is guarded by whispering gulls.

Raven listens, whistling in stunted trees.

ANITA ENDREZZE-PROBST

THE PASSION DRINKER

"Their horses will sink into the earth.
The riders will jump from their horses
but they will sink into the earth also."

—Short Bull
Moon of Falling Leaves
1890

When he was young, he broke horses.
They sweated, trembled, kneeled.
He boxed their noses, cut off their breath;
foam, bloody and thick, lathered his hands.
Slim Girl watched from cracked railings,
perched like a small laughing bird.

Once, in the National Finals, he rode
Tornado Devil to the finish time.
When his hand got caught in the ropes,
his leg bent, and splintered.
He took the girl and moved to the city.
Now, hunched in smoky rooms, he has visions.

His lame arms grope, reaching for Spitfire.
Horses breathe like past lovers in his dreams.
Slim Girl guides his hand, from table
to glass, to mouth. Her fingers are singing.
The moon has fallen into his bottle.
He is comforted; it is a second tongue.

He hears Wovoka's voice announcing
the next event. Short Bull is out
in the Badlands; the Messiah is Indian.
The Ghost Dancers raise their arms to stop

bullets, while the audience applauds for more.
The charging horses stink of sulfur.

The woman's lap is filled with his hands,
calming him. He is collecting bones
of milky flowers, smelling hollowed cones.
Foxes dance in tunnels, moles curl
their skinny paws around starry threads
of buried ghost shirts. In his visions,

The passion drinker thinks he's seen it all,
But the dead say only the earth endures.

RED ROCK CEREMONIES

> The clear moon arcs
> over the sleeping Three Sisters,
> like the conchos that string
> the waist of a dancer.

With low thunder, with red bushes smooth
as water stones, with the blue-arrowed rain,
its dark feathers curving down
and the white-tailed running deer—
the desert sits, a maiden with obsidian eyes,
brushing the star-tassled dawn from her lap.

It is the month of Green Corn;
It is the dance, Grandfather, of open blankets.

> I am singing to you
> I am making the words
> shake like bells.

Owl Woman is blessing all directions.
This corn—with its leaves that are yellow
in the sun, with the green of small snakes,
with its Mother Earth's hair and even teeth,
with its long leaves, its dark stem,
and the small blue bird that drinks from its roots—
you are shaking purple in dusk,
you are climbing the rims of the world.

Old Grandfather, we are combing your hair
for blue stars and black moons.
With white corn, with cloud feathers,
you are crossing dawn without the Dream Runners.

I am closing your blanket
I am making the words
    speak in circles.

THE WEEK-END INDIAN

I

In red wool jacket and earflaps
you circle your camp three times
before you realize you're lost.
You deny it, squinting at moss
growing on the north of trees,
and thumb through your new copy
of "Indian Lore and Camp Book."
The pages are blank.

Your compass, with its glowing digits,
whirs spastically toward your feet.
Fur-lined and waterproofed, your boots

are, in case of emergencies, edible.
Your fishing line has become knotted,
clumped in a thick-leafed bush,
like a small bird's nest.
The redwoods gather above you,
waiting like many-winged vultures:
Your panic is dead meat at their claws.

Lost, on the night of your first day,
you huddle against a deep cliff
whispering into your palms,
cupping them against your ears.
They answer you in slow echoes.

2

Morning.
Survival drums in your pulse.
What was it your ancestors knew?
Listen.
In the sounds of water falling,
you hear the soft voices of women:

> "We each are called Fear,
> we all lie on our backs—
> we are salmon returning to spawn
> pink-fleshed in your streams.
> We soon die."

Silence! Silence! You shout them quiet.
Small noises make you jump.
The forest is shifting its weight for you.
You build reed shrines in hollow crevices,
digging into the earth with your knees.
Scanning the sky for your rescue,

your eyes are scratched by branches.
Silence crawls into your skin like maggots.

3
On the third day, the cold earth
measures your body.
It accepts you.
Your fear pushes you deeper.
The firs reach for your shoulders,
matching limb with limb.
You eat dust,
sucking stones like a child.
Games lurk in the corners
of your eyes: Someone is stalking you.
You feel your back bristle, twigs snap,
your neck aches. When you turn around,
no one is there.
You assume it isn't human.

When you gaze slack-eyed at the sky,
you see her. Her face is a cloud.
This Indian woman you left
with nothing whispers:
I let my blood be known.
You can feel her blood follow you,
like a hungry animal.

4
On the fourth day,
you can go no further.
She is satisfied.
Her voice rakes you like a bear's claws.
She teaches you your death song;

ANITA ENDREZZE-PROBST

There are no words, only howling.
What she has to say is enough:

"The ponds, thick with murmuring fish,
defy your limit. The ones you threw away
have given me voice. Listen!
Deep in survival, the fish are churning
the waters, they are climbing the rocks,
speckled, flicking foam,
floating in banked wedges, belly up.

I follow them as they tally their dead
and they are speaking of you.
Buried in wet leaves, your love falls apart
like the swollen soft bodies
of white-sided fish.
    Lost one, I am filling my hands
    with the depths of your grave.
    I let my blood be known.
    I will not paint my face white.
    Look! The Fish women have changed.
    Around me, they are ravens,
    swallowing winged serpents.
    They are picking your bones:
    they are naming you silent."

When she is finished,
her words surround you like chill winds.

                    5
On the last day, the earth heaves
its gullies to cover your quiet body.
Ten years from now, playing children
will find your root-thin bones
shattered against buried rocks.

Voices of the Rainbow

They will wonder about survival
during blind winters
that crack bones like jammed ice.
They will wonder what happened
and when, but in the end,
they will say nothing,
thinking it to be only
the grave of an animal.

THE DREAM FEAST   *(Three Poems)*

1
The Sleeper's Song

The thrust of the dragon's tight bone
deepens the wound: His tongue switchblades
the moon-drugged sleeper.

    (I am eating my stomach)

The woman who screams without voice
picks the teeth of my dreams.

    (I am wiping my lips)

At certain times of the year,
the sea vomits blood.

2
The Dragon's Dream

The dragon's dream fires tongues
of coiling snakes: Scale burning scale,

smoke rising like an oracle.
In silence, the sphinx asks.

The question has never been needed.
The screaming woman gave birth to daggers
too beautiful to resist blood.
My spiked tail whips her stern lips.

The sphinx has eyes of crystal.
When I look into them, I see myself
within a halo of dreams.

3
The Feast

The sphinx, denied a voice,
turns to stone: the teeth of her vagina
knife through my riddled dreams.

    (Too swollen with blood to rise)

Inside her, I am clenching the dragon.
He is a sleeping worm, curled in a congealing sea.

    (The moon is mired in my flesh)

The crouching sphinx swallows my name.
At her smile, the feast begins.

Charles Ballard

(QUAPAW/CHEROKEE)

THEIR CONE-LIKE CABINS

"Their cone-like cabins," she said
That poetess of Hartford
Who gently took her stick
Sweetly stirred the ashes
Of Hiawatha's book

"Ye say they went away," she sang
The Winnebago certainly did
About seven times
And at every stopping place
The same old words

As long as rivers flow
And grass shall grow
The strong will stuff their pockets
Usually break wind
As they calmly watch you go

GRANDMA FIRE

Grandma Fire
Old and naked in the dawn
No answer sings out from your lips
Only the kettle deep
Ferment of tribes   fires that keep
To the edge of night
Old hands like roots
But seedlings to life   birds to wing!

Grandma Fire
Every way on that time
Eyes appeared from every stream
People seemed to flee
Headstrong the wind   strong the fire
From every hand it was
Crisscrossing the land
And gone it was   birds to wing!

Grandma Fire
Always ours for the good
The songs were ours to sing
Twisting, barking in the flood
From every forest   from deeper spring
Where rooted everlasting
The Indian heart
And ever uplifting   birds to wing!

MEMO

It would be painful to interfere
To set the locust among the corn

Voices of the Rainbow

118

To set the tiger upon the lamb
To set man against fellow man
To adjust the conquest, oversee the plan
To let a nation fall and proclaim
White death and cold and bitterness
While leaders like dry twigs are cast
Into the fire by those who rub
Their hands and smile . . .
It would be painful to interfere

THE SPIRIT CRAFT

How beautiful and calm how crimson pale
And sweet the dawn upon God's mountainside
Tomorrow is here if we but decide
To see it through step lightly through the veil
From darkness to the day let spirit sail
Across the night and feel the sway and glide
Of spirit craft when word and deed provide
The passage sure upward into the light

Today is now a yesterday a line
Unbroken from joyous youth through a dream
Of enfeebled age a spring and waterfall
A river winding broad and deep across the plain
A memory of mountains and a stream
That always was from out of heaven's wall

CHARLES BALLARD

THE SPEAKER

You are less than one-half
Of one per cent of the total population

Who is he kidding?

Anomalous feather on the massive chain
We sweep toward the sea as live remains
Fatalists to the end, to the end!
Dare I say *Indian?*
Die in a thicket, pink-looking man
With dollar bills up to your chin
Up there behind the podium

The dead will not return, in any season
And I see the game—to blow the mind
Puff up the name, and multiply
Beyond all reason
But what one does to the world, little brother
Is run it as best he can, all of us
Up there behind the podium

Say rather this—

To live with the fox
Is to build in the mind
What comes first, what comes last
And to hide nothing
Except yourself

When the fox rules the land
All trails will be safe
No bones will you find
Far in the forest dim they lie
Only for his eye

THE WINDS OF CHANGE

In the eye of seafaring man
You began as thyme or sprig
A minty taste, a godly word
A heaven beyond the Baltic

When Allegory was king
You rode a horse, began to sing
A monk in robes on flowered fields
And quite secure in your strength

Countless minds from that time
And countless lips both bright
And dim have shaped your sound
In the world of men

What are you now? What were you then?
An obscenity of late—did you know?
Ran through the streets, a twisted shape
None could explain nor tried

Too long against the winds of change
What once was only thyme or sprig
Another world will slowly fade
Pass, then, into oblivion, sweet word

NOW THE PEOPLE HAVE THE LIGHT

Now the people have the light
But time must pass, days of autumn
While the deer drank at the pool

CHARLES BALLARD

Visions gathered by proud men
Will not affect the light, the summer rains
Must fall on a world of leaves

The swarms of small life on wings
Must find the lake, the evening birds
Bring back the songs of youth

Steaming riverbeds on the Great Plains
Must sigh for the lizard and receive
In dark sand the wayward stars

Mountain peaks high over the land
Must keep the watch through all the years
For now the people have the light

YOU NORTHERN GIRL

You northern girl, be yet
The fine sand along the River Platte
Blue flames along hickory logs
Above the ground where dancers dance

South to the yellow world
The amber world of morning lakes
Long-stemmed stillness that seldom breaks
Nor disturbs the sun's resting place

Small birds have not the wings for this
The flight across time and unlocked rhythms
Nor are they as pebbles in a stream
With colors drawn deep from wintry days

You northern girl, speak yet
Of a time of many trees, many camps of the strong
Mountain peaks that guard the fertile land
The purer light now lost to man

Though in the furnace of the Southlands
Deep in the city's web we meet
We will wing our way to the River Platte
Toward the fires of our Indian world

SAND CREEK

Wild bird singer, sing on!

Nothing lives long
But the earth and the mountain
What remains in the fire, in the flames
Becomes the final song

Listen hard to the words
From the winter's whiteness they come
And on this day too old to run am I
Too old for the land of the young

Black Kettle raises the flag
The air is crisp and cold
Here at my home I sing
Nothing lives long
But the earth and the mountain

White Antelope is my name

CHARLES BALLARD

DURING THE PAGEANT
AT MEDICINE LODGE

During the pageant at Medicine Lodge
One bright line this—recollected but passing away,
      like a leaf that escaped the fire; it
      appears still golden, life-inhabited,
      imbued with light, with the filtered hush
      of deep forests.

During the pageant at Medicine Lodge
Later it seemed that the redman had been only a dream
      on paper, an elegant falsehood strutting
      before pioneers, a dancing image fading
      deeper into the forests, into the wild streams,
      into earth itself. They were never real!
      They sang—bird-like, bear-like, like wind,
      rustle of trees, crickets—and were no more.

During the pageant at Medicine Lodge
Conversational scraps and ideas. "A few might have
      survived," I said. I wanted to say,
      "You and I." But why stab at thin air.
      The past survives in the mind. On that
      particular day in southern Kansas *no Indians*
      were there. It was a jolly ride, it was dusty
      and hot, it was fun, but the Indians,
      whoever they were, did not arrive.

Ramona Wilson

(COLVILLE)

KEEPING HAIR   *1973*

My grandmother had braids
at the thickest, pencil wide
held with bright wool
cut from her bed shawl.
No teeth left but white hair
combed and wet carefully
early each morning.
The small wild plants found among stones
on the windy and brown plateaus
revealed their secrets to her hand
and yielded to her cooking pots.
She made a sweet amber water
from willows,
boiling the life out
to pour onto her old head.
"It will keep your hair."
She bathed my head once

rain water not sweeter.
The thought that once
when I was so very young
her work-bent hands
very gently and smoothly
washed my hair in willows
may also keep my heart.

OVERNIGHT GUEST   *1973*

Do you know that once
when you thought I was asleep
you passed naked by my door
the street light came in white
to show the curve
and long dizzying line
of your back
imagining that curve
to this night.

READING INDIAN POETRY   *1974*

Once we dreamed of eagles,
the scurrying flights of black bears
beckoning tails of deer
white in the darkness of noon woods,
but we see instead the road's dust
rising slowly into the dead sky
has smothered and discolored

all that lies beside.
The chicken hawks wheel far and small.
We are grateful for them.
Fat, cold-eyed crows lighten our day.

SUMMER

1973

firefly light
        the only movement
in trees
        dark with summer weighted silence
a lullaby from some bird
        long expanse of grass
where it is not hard to lie
        moon burned with flame
when the sun goes
we smell for the first time in years
quiet clover, lilac trees,
a belief
        in small things aware
of our slight and hesitant moves
        as we turn
the moon is so bright
the light bursts within me.

EVENINGSONG 1

1973

willow leaves dancing
I shall remember forever that I live

RAMONA WILSON

127

the shadows across the evening
orange lighting your cheeks
the softening and darkening of your eyes
as we leaned toward the promise
silent, the time stretching away
the violet hill having no horizon
time like the ripple on ripple
of leaves in a chorus
on the trees we loved
in the rhythm of our bodies
oh, our bodies dance
do you remember the dance
bending to music from our knees
the sunlit day long in shadows
already showing the last light
in the grass long and nodding.

EVENINGSONG 2   *1973*

during one period I remember
you made poems all day
by breakfast one
and by evening enough to light our table.
anticipating the sun
we would leave our beds instantly
no regret
days to watch the lazy fish
the ever-singing birds
to crawl under vines an hour
for a handful of sweetness
to watch the river without melancholy

the deep green water slow
as the arch of the daily sun
to watch the evening come with only shouts
ticklish games behind grass.
now the crickets are monotonous
the fish have long since decayed.
twilight comes
we light all the lamps.

LATE IN FALL   *1973*

To love November, a turned joy
in new strength of sight
a view unbroken, no ornaments
obstructions of blown rose
but bones of the bush, bareness of weed
essential at last caressed
finally to dip my heart in stream disclosed
new buildings unguilty as the land,
is a delight in birds, no longer hiding
singing on fine and shivering limbs
of spread and open trees.

THE MEETING   *1974*

feel the sharpness
the familiar pain of this end
our anticipated fall,
our reward being quietness.

I laugh again
listening to the turns
of our meeting, my love,
but reluctantly
for know I dispense
fragments of freedom
collected with effort,
shards of reasonable nights.

SPRING IN VIRGINIA   *1974*

Come, let us walk
Winter has lost again.
Flickers flash and celebrate
the way our hands touch.
The river swells, a curve,
the sun smooths and shines your mouth.

SPRING AT FORT OKANOGAN   *1974*

Thought I heard the wind,
closed my eyes to see
those old lovers, the rivers
coming together at last
pushing down from Canada,
rivers Columbia and Okanogan
down southward to meet in whirling
and festivities of the marriage
of waters, one green

and one sky-hard gray
and throwing aside, as gestures of joy
celebrating the coming consummation
of sea, pacificness,
bluebells and babyfaces, roses
mustard flowers
and paeaning, the wind
the wind named Chinook.
Chinook, urges of salmon, early plowing
the earth dark in hollows.
Again in northwest spring
the Chinook is gathering itself
again rising strong.
The air will be sweet
as breath of new horses.

BAGS PACKED AND WE EXPECTED THIS

1974

Let us say good-bye
again and again
for the rose blooms
on a cold spring day

We can prolong it
repeat and repeat
wake to see the moon
hard and full

We can forget
and not hear the petal fall
when the moon is loveliest
it is not called new

Voices of the Rainbow

Come again
though our clocks sing
though the sun races
in the end we do but sleep.

A. K. Redwing

(SIOUX)

SITTING BULL'S WILL VERSUS THE SIOUX TREATY OF 1868 AND MONTY HALL

1

Clarence Short Bull died.

the bullet was aimed decades ago
by a finger from Washington
whose brain is kept alive, in a tank of formaldehyde,
    by electrodes . . .

His body laid in state
behind the "Jiffy Wash Launderette" for two hundred years

a janitor, a passing wino,
and a cockroach noticed . . .

2

A thick haze gloves the scene

like smoke
from the campfires of a million homeless landlords

Embedded in it are
counterfeit IOUs, an 8 x 10 glossy of Daffy Duck
in Indian drag, a small pock,

and a vast army of granite-faced clowns.

CHROME BABIES EATING CHOCOLATE
SNOWMEN IN THE MOONLIGHT

1

In Chu hai, dead machine guns lie frozen in the sun
        rotting and forgotten they lie—
horrible smelling and ever present . . .
                Smack shrunken
teddy bears stumble blindly
            from twisted barrels

on another S and D mission, they creep
            past silent villages
like intelligent puppets

2

A perturbed sun peeks cautiously over the Px skyline
            startled moonbeams,
fearing death, seek shelter behind a smacked out
            platoon of rapists and hitmen

3

A group of touring politicians is shown an elaborate
    Ball of Chicanery—
"Brilliant," said the Bozo from Wazoo . . .
"A commendable piece of artistry," said another.

A. K. REDWING

135

> they continue on their tour
of freshly polished commodes . . .
playing their role of blind men at a silent movie

    4

An August eagle floats majestically across the sky,
> He is met by a SAM II . . .

the feathers land selectively in living rooms
> from Maine to Seattle . . .

TWO HOOKERS

    I

reeking of unsolved crime, the cop
> pursues a flat-footed junkie
>> into a bottomless garbage can
Following a brief exchange of animosities
>> they emerge . . .
the cop wearing sandals and a thousand bills
> the junkie, a badge and 24 lumps

    2

>>> two hookers
kneel in the shadow of a mafia boss . . .
> the money in their hands once
>> belonged to the pope

    3

>>> a cosmic jury
finds the true villains of wounded knee guilty. . . .

a plowshare and a reaper
hang at dawn—
A radio, a television set, and a bourgeois
prairie newspaper hang as accomplices

WRITTEN IN UNBRIDLED REPUGNANCE
NEAR SIOUX FALLS, ALABAMA—
APRIL 30, 1974

1

As the dust from the wet dream of a nation
settles on the tuxedoes
of yesterday's heroes,

a friendly hand becomes a fist

forged in elusive furnaces
by unseen Hitlers, in ignorance. . . .

2

While eternally sightless eyes compete
with hopelessly deaf ears for

the first crack at your ass,

the beast in the living room
winks its psychedelic orb
at a picture of Chief Joseph. . . .

3

Bronze statues of ancient rapists
applaud tactical squads crunching skulls

A. K. REDWING

137

As in the dim light of humanity,

Adam weeps. . . .

TORNADO SOUP

the Wino was eating soup
     like an event that never happened. . . .

Abused eyes catalogued me as
     a drop of soup slithered through the stubble

to join yesterday's Italian Swiss
     on his forgotten wardrobe. . . .

                    I smiled.
"A bank president on his lunch break,"
                    I said.

A BLUE JEANED ROCK QUEEN IN SEARCH OF HAPPINESS ON A BLIND THURSDAY AT 1/3 SPEED AND CRYING

   In the elbow of a macaroni
my identity lurks . . .

          like an unemployed idea
pretending it's a drop of rain.

THE HOOFER

Passing like a Strauss waltz
        before your eyes
the butterfly clicks its heels
in time to a much higher music.

AGENT OF LOVE

Carrying generations of lust on his tiny feet,
      the yellow jacket buzzes
over lovers fornicating breathlessly in the fields

COSMIC EYE

A clear, noon sky at midsummer is God's eye;
      the sun is the light shining from within and
you are an episode of life under constant scrutiny.

A LOST MOHICAN VISITS
HELL'S KITCHEN

Hopelessly handcuffed to a mysterious butterfly,
      we bump elbows in the supermarket

and drink sad spirits through
      "You can't get something for nothing" daydreams.

A. K. REDWING

139

THE WORLD'S LAST UNNAMED POEM

In an Indiana ditch lies
　　a deer with one antler missing. . . .

　　　　　　Broken by a runaway
2oth Century,
　　he lies with a philosophical expression
etched in blood. . . .

there is a surplus salute,
　　　　left over from a repressed war,
in Duc Pho, S. Viet Nam. . . .

A dotted line connects
　　　　　　　　the missing antler with
the left-over salute

Somewhere . . .
　　　　in an unknown era . . .
there is someone who understands why . . .

we do the things we do.

Peter Blue Cloud

(M O H A W K)

HAWK NAILED TO A BARN DOOR

December 23, 1973

Hawk nailed to a barn door,
and rain makes you small and dark, and my muddy boots
are ankle-deep in ground fog,
far away dog barks sharp as cracking rifles
disked earth the hayfield's primal mud
        your brother and sister rough-legged hawks
of quick-beating wings and spread, down-pointed tails
momentarily transfixed in air as if fighting
        an up-slanting gale from earth.
Hobbling with practiced dignity, Chauncy, my new dog neighbor
with casts on front legs, limps forward
        to good-morning me the day, hesistant.
Yes, I am trying to fashion a scene to forget the maggots
and the stink, your hollow eaten eyes and tight closed
talons in last grasping, nailed through wing muscles,
head down to side, crucified,
        curved beak slightly open to my own questions

who has lost another particle of faith.
                    Your wings and claws dry now above the stove,
and the rising heat gently revolves them.
It is 4:30 a.m. and cold and dark and your feathers
will be passed on to sky lovers.
                    I was choking slightly, deep down, as I removed
your wings, claws, and tail feathers, then one by one
I took a handful of breast down,
                    so warm looking.
Buried you behind the barn with two pepperwood leaves
and a mumbled se-sa-ton-ti, o-nen,
                    go-home, now
Sat down in anger for your senseless murder,
all set to write a bitter song,
                    it is 5:00 a.m. now
and your feathers so close send me no messages of hate.
I look at your beautiful wings
                    and sense your flight.

WOLF   *January 28, 1974*

burrowing deep into earth until the grave is complete,
hiding in daytime shadows, panting,
                              sweat,
          dry matted blood
          and stump of a leg,
wolf, his growls into whimpers of pain unending.

she-wolf keening the stiffened, frozen cubs,
licking the frosted muzzles cyanide tracings,
                              sweet

Voices of the Rainbow
142

the steaming meat
she gently places
as an offering, though she knows they are dead.

run down to earth and snow with bursting heart,
down to the bright red hammering pulse, and further

                                    down

      one by one
      the rifle shot
echo resounding a terrible, alien blood lust.

protruding blackened tongues, no more the night chant,
blanket of sound, the earth her moaning,
                        futile,
      her emptied womb,
      and the seed
dried and rustling among forgotten leaves.

             *

a wind of running leaves across the prairie,
a scent of pine in frozen north the muskeg
      lakes
            lent footprints
      cast in sandstone
grains rubbing time the desert's constant edge.

softly contoured voices moaning night,
the wolves in circle council the moon
      shadows
            bent starlight
      of fingered sleet
rattles the gourd of earth down feathered roots.

PETER BLUE CLOUD

143

beyond beginnings the earth her many tribes
and clans their life songs merge into one
      chant
            welcome dance
     to the unborn
awaiting birth in the sun-fingered dawn.

and to each creation the heartline trail
is etched in delicate memory pattern
      webs
            so intricate
     in a unity
of day into night the seasons follow.

the moaning low of wolves to ears of men
first wisdom gained by another's quiet
      song
            of meditation
     circle of council
bound together by their basic power.

and the quiet way of learning was the food
and spark the hearth of compassion warm
      enfolding
            all others
     born of earth
in the harmony of mutual need.

in thanks the minds of curious men
sought further wisdom from the brother
      wolf
            his clan
     a social order
of strength through lasting kinship.

Voices of the Rainbow

and recognized the she-wolf's place
in balance with that of the male leader
        heads
                of family
        to be obeyed
because their first law was survival.

and studied the pattern of the hunt
where each had a particular role
        defined
                by need
        and acted upon
without the slightest hesitation.

and moaning low the wolf song
head bent the drummer and voice to sky
        singer
                in thanks
        to brother wolf,
now your song we will sing in our voices.

                *

again the rifle shot and snapping jaws
of steel traps and poisoned bait,
the bounty hunter and fur trapper
        predators
        of greed
whose minds create vast lies.

and moaning low in death chant
the one remaining wolf staggers
        and falls
        to death
as winds carry his voice into tomorrow.

and the voice is an accusation howling
within the brain heart pulling sinews
      harshly,
      you, too,
I hang my death about your neck in circle.

mourn the buffalo and the beaver,
keen the fox and mountain cat,
      shout
      the grizzly
antelope elk moose caribou and many

more gone into death the prime breeders
to fashion garments of vanity,
      Indian,
      brother,
cleanse the blood lust from your naked spirit

and fast and pray your spirit's new growth
and be reborn into childhood innocence
      purity
      our maker
awaits your ancient promise.

the wolf in dream has petitioned
for his voice to be heard in council
      now
      in this place
let us open our minds.

          *

scattered and lost the people fall,
orphaned, the child feels hunger,
      where is tomorrow,

where does it hide?
there are four voices coming
from four directions
        the center is harmony,
        the center is beginning.
scouts and messengers called back,
the council is the mind
        it is merging thought
        the nation's birth.
now, when warriors feast,
they eat of embers
        the fire's heat
        stored energy.
the warrior society
is the wolf society
        is the clan family
        heart of tribe.
anger seeking wisdom,
council after meditation
        there is a vision
        held in sacred trust.

                    *

I dance upon my three remaining legs,
                            look,
the memory of the fourth keeps my balance,
                                    see,
my wispy white and cyanide fog-breath,
                            hah!
taut sinews vibrate the sky's held thunder,
                            huh!
steel traps I weave a necklace of your making,

                                        hah!
puffs of dust I quick-stomp with paw feet,
                                    huh!
I am becoming you dancing for them,
                                hah!
I jump upon your back a heavy robe,
                                huh!
my shadow will nip your pumping ankle,
                                    huh!
you will think you me in the full moon night,
                                    huh!
I crush your long bones sucking marrow,
nose your severed head before me the trail,
tear strips of flesh the ribbons weave a net,
chew hair and fingernails into mash
I slap upon my festered stump your human glue,
                                    hah!
now you are dancing,
                brother,
                        now you are dancing.

SWEAT SONG

coyote
    running
running
    coyote

deserts
    of ice
rivers
    crystal pain

PETER BLUE CLOUD

mountains
 breathing
  coyote

sweat bath
 cedar shadow
mirror hawk
 dream feel
coyote coyote
 obsidian claws
hey, coyote
 hey, coyote

roundhouse
 of coyote
mountains
 breathing
mirror hawk
 hey, coyote
cedar shadow
 hey, coyote
coyote
 running
running
 coyote
song
 done.

DEATH CHANT

buffalo, buffalo, buffalo, buffalo
 running

thundering
stampede
quenching life

slaughtered
we die the buffalo
slaughtered
we die
the buffalo
slaughtered
the buffalo
we die

butchered
my song continues
grizzly, grizzly, grizzly, grizzly
O, bear
O, turtle
I sing.

COMPOSITION

there was the buffalo blowing
blood and steam from throat wound
and even the smell of gore and
of fear mingling hate anger,
the sound of the great heart
thumping,
and a leg convulsively pawing
a furrow,
and already
the first flies,

the hunter's desperate pull
upon the short thrusting spear,
                          ashamed
of his poor aim
                  causing such pain
     to his brother,
desperately
     wanting to plunge again
                          true,
to end mutual pain,
and the horse standing trembling
and frothing from the wild
     ecstasy of the chase,
     and a plain,
and mountains and glorious clouds,
all such a rich canvas,
     and beyond the easel
                          a bare
     white wall
and the inner image of a composition
     beyond manipulation.

UNTITLED

walking through twisted hollow pathways
hand in hand under blue
sky tracings of wispy question
marks the flight of gulls
and this land is green and this land
trembles with old and young
lovers loose-footing adventure

into golden autumns and winter
cabins the wood smoke sharp

bite of axe to tree to ground
the sting of sweat a pungent odor
of climbing hills the deer's delicate
steps to stars the universe of grasses
bared to swaying breezes the likes
of elderberry flutes melodious
quivering fingers of sound the lap
and shush of gentle waves on sand
the lake a turquoise feast platter
overflowing with an abundance

of many flavored delicacies
savored the tang of rootlets
plucked from mud the pond
awaiting the evening loon's
practiced mirror laughter
the chuckling canoe cutting
waters the river directs to sea
and harbors close the salmon
spawn a million tiny eyes
direct the passage of the sun

to mountain's unseen mystery
stories recited upon a feather's down
flight the eagle stone thrown
to ground the twang of bowstring

vibration of wings the hummingbird
slapped tail shout of echoes the beaver
sniffs the otter's nose cruising by
willows their roots entangling
dream flights their arrow leaves

spear sunlight in shadow flecks
dappled the frog coat and croak
bristling fur the wolverine dances
sideways and around fallen antlers
of oak trees and sugarpine first frost
the valleys crack and split back
and forth the saws of crickets
night song again the bullfrog
bass bellow the lilypad chewings
snout glistening moose twitching
ears the child buffalo bawling
tentative tangle of unsteady legs
stiffened now the hunter's poise
upon tears blurring aim and deed
and deed the earth to brother wolf
teeth grinding corn the grandmother
sings rabbit songs the grandchild
forgetting owl's warnings hooted
the cradle song of night worlds
without end the stars dance across
sky path the night hawks sacred
shadows within shadows deep
furry chirping chitters the fallen tree

of moss and memories hanging
tangled hair the ancient cedar
raven roost and wonderment
the dawn's first dove cooing
rocks the gentle cradle breeze
faint embers the fire's warmth
breathes the newday glorious
orange, red, purple, blue
and giggles the child awakened
      into day.

Phil George

(NEZ PERCÉ / TSIMSHIAN)

Dedication:
      Descendants of the War of 1877
      Chief Joseph Band of Nez Percé
      Colville Reservation, Washington State

PRELUDE TO MEMORIAL SONG

100 Years Later

Before an audible sound, an almost recognizable
Tune: a puppy cry—a whimper from my heart.
My withheld burst of air pierces morning stillness.
Up, up misty Nespelem Cascades where
Eagles and Salmon two-step on rainbows.

Coyote licks my tears; I sing.
Steam rises from Owhi Lake and I sing.
For long time ago freedom I am lonely, so lonely.
amerika's-whiteman-life makes me sad.
Am I alone?
Puplukhh (Grandfather) is dead.
Kautsa (Grandmother) is dead.

Prisoners of war home from Oklahoma concentration
Camps in OUR OWN COUNTRY.
        Finally dead.
Inside I bleed.
        I hurt.
        I hurt.
        I hurt.

Their Life Song, a portage for my spirit,
Traces glacial springs to the mountainside.
With morning vapors my heart will rise—
When red and yellow plumes dance down between pines
My heavy heart will rise.

I am alive.
Nemipu are breathing humans:

        We
                Are
                        Alive.

THE VISIT

Grandmother, I dreamed of you again—
I burned the sage you
        sent when I was in Vietnam.
Before you died—
        and I could not come home.
Beside my bed is the Spruce Bough
        to keep nightmares away.

Today I will visit you beside
        Our Stream—at Arrow.

I will sprinkle tobacco on waters:
    They will thank me.

Grandmother, let's visit—
    Talk and laugh when
    Sun is shining;
So I may sleep, rest at night.

SUNFLOWER MOCCASINS

Spring, and a new pair of moccasins!
These: floral beaded,
    with sky-blue, Happiness, background.

Now, I must race through
    Buttercup meadows
    and bring a gift of
Flowers of the Sun to
Grandmother for celery.

When the leaves change their colors
    She changes my moccasins
      as she pleases.

AMERICA'S WOUNDED KNEE

(an unpoetic subject on assignment)

First full moon of overgrown Buffalo Grass;
Missionary, settler, squatter.
Progress, they call it—they call it progress.

PHIL GEORGE

157

"Your past is best forgotten," says McGovern.
Justified genocide, not manslaughter,
And Medicine Man Crow Dog is imprisoned.
Trials begun with no "Injuns" on jury.

For seventy-one days the tepee stood,
Their solitary lodge, beside the church.
One more remains—just one per cent left.

SPRING CLEANING

What is that growling! Screeching! Barking!
As if animals are fighting in the closet?

I must air out the regalia—
Shirts, horse trappings, buffalo hides, warbonnets.

Otters, wolves, ermine, porcupine, deer
And eagles need a breath of spring air too.

I must air out the regalia.

SPRUCE

She transplanted each spruce, blue as the
Blue Mountains from where they came.
Laden with child in womb, on horseback she went,
Bareback and alone—overnight.
Her floral-beaded saddlebags with fringes to hooves
Were filled with the last salmon run—smoked, sweet—
And the freshest of broiled venison.

In our little Switzerland, private and "undiscovered,"
She made an opening in the forest;
She sang in the Sun where she uprooted the tree.
She planted each spruce—one for each child—
Seven healthy trees, strong in a row.
Except one.
That was Uncle in Korea.
She knew the second he was wounded when
She detected yellow fungus on the bleeding bark.
Under Uncle's arm she slept until the telegram came.

In mourning she cut off her braids;
She planted them under the fungus—it disappeared.
She planted the telegram under his roots
Just like she planted salmon in the hole she
Dug with deer antlers when she planted each spruce.
Salmon returns to its same spawning stream
To die.

Anthropologists study our "pagan spruce worship"—
Evergreen ferns that carry Smoke Prayers eternally skyward—
And wonder . . . "Why?"
Sophisticated vultures in the shade of her spruce
Eating their lunch after picking our bones
And pulling her braids . . . laughing.

And I wonder: Why?

FAVORITE GRANDSON BRAID

I do not think Grandmother or Grandfather
    had a favorite grandson.

PHIL GEORGE

159

But still, with special care I weave
      three long strands above my left temple.

Favorite Grandson Braid touches my heart.

NAME GIVEAWAY

That teacher gave me a new name . . . again.
      She never even had feasts or a giveaway!

Still I do not know what "George" means;
      and now she calls me: "Phillip."

          TWO SWANS ASCENDING FROM STILL WATERS
      must be a name too hard to remember.

MOON OF HUCKLEBERRIES

Black Bear sang, drumming on a log:
"Come, bring your biggest baskets
To the best berry patches.
      I'll show you.

"If you maidens get lost—
Just follow my dung.
Just follow my dung."
Black Bear sang, drumming on a log.

FIRST GRADE

From moccasins to shoes—
    Unsteady steps,
Unwilling to unlearn
    Old Ways.

SPOKANE FALLS

In vain Her veins incised—jagged boulders—
Earth's entrails tossed about,
Choice stones stolen to build
A "chapel" they called it.

Vermin anglos have murdered their jesus
And now they have come to kill our Gods.

Palms calloused or raw to bones,
Our backs humped from lifting, lifting.
With sorrow eyes, our heads were high.
Sun Father shines: Our shadows ARE ours.

Whipped! punished, or shot running if we
Dared to defy those black-robed priests.

Thunder and Waters went raging mad!
Vomiting white venom in floods—drowning
That cold, vile coffin of hypocrisy.
Our River Shrine was almost altered.

But, what a waste of rocks
For that "chapel," they called it.

PHIL GEORGE

161

WARDANCE

When you wardance, sometimes you must
Move like a bird—disguised in eagle feathers
    and secret fetishes.

And your enemies will fear
    This medicine movement of time and space—

Especially Christian Indians allied with calvary;
    They are really scared!

MORNING VIGIL

Each morning the birds awake me;
    they sing up the Sun—
In silence I watch; I listen.
    That's the only respect I can offer.

My little feathered brothers and sisters
    know it's not easy to be
An Indian in a strange world . . .
They sing to me:
    Endure!
    Be Strong!

My little friends and I will endure.
While the whole world sleeps,
    We endure.
    We sing.

WARDANCE SOUP

This evening I prepared Wardance Soup
    before the Many Trails Powwow.

Her recipe was the same:
    boiled stew meat
    wild onions
    sprinkled flour and salt

Somehow, Grandmother's flavor
    of singing and her pinewood fire
    was something special
I could not add.

"Ya-Ka-Nes" / Patty L. Harjo

(SENECA/SEMINOLE)

DEATH   *October 1971*

Ancientness surrounds me
Loneliness creeps in through my ears
Growing very old until there is no movement—
No sound—only waiting
Sitting
An invisible spirit
Watching

WISHES   *September 1972*

Over the rainy day mountain
Past the laughing blue rainbow
Gliding in the cloudless ivory sky
The young Happiness bird
In the freedom of quiet solitude or

with a loved-one friend
Always follow the beauty road
Gliding in the cloudless ivory sky
Past the laughing blue rainbow
Over the rainy day mountain
Forever in happiness
Forever in beauty
Always

TAOS WINTER

January 1971

Sound of happy laughter leap with shadows on the walls.
The woven sunset colors a closeness to nature.
Sings . . . the happy water—it is life
Warmth . . . the fire—it is love
Shine . . . the star—it is beauty
Quiet night . . . I must—stop—look—listen
Singing life—Warm love—Shining beauty
A place to be lonely for.

THE MASK

While upon the journey of life
I found a mask lying beside
The winding road
I bent down

In jest placed it upon my brow
Then, I saw the world

"YA-KA-NES"/PATTY L. HARJO

In all its ugliness
And I cried

WHERE HAVE YOU GONE, LITTLE BOY

Denver, Colorado, June 4, 1971

Where have you gone, Little Boy,
with the Elfen smile?
Where did you go yesterday?
Do your eyes still outshine the stars?
Does your voice whisper softer than the wind?
Where have we gone from Yesterday?
When i left you there was no smile, no stars, or
words.
i gave you no understanding Yesterday.
Each day i remember and wonder if you still
remember our Yesterdays
Little Boy with the Elfen smile my very first love
If i should see you again, will you give me more
Yesterdays from your tomorrows?

TO AN INDIAN POET

May 1969

Close to nature my brother, your thoughts ring softly on
the quiet air.
You speak of sunrise, the hunt and your animal soul.
    I sat on the floor of my lodge and my heart is filled
with pride.
I look upon the face of your mother, I listen to your words,

I see a tear steal from her shining eyes and I am
happy too.

As your voice becomes silent, your memory speaks loud
to my soul.

This night you have given me much happiness to carry
within an empty heart.

Lew Blockcolski

(C H E R O K E E / C H O C T A W)

RESERVATION SPECIAL

The man with the camera comes,
whirling black metal knobs, while
yelling chief commands, unanointed.
Aiming his one-eyed magic
he frames headroaches and cockroaches.
Separating houses from the land,
he plots Indian plight
with pre-answered questions.
Then he stuffs his black bag
with our lives and is gone
in his alphabet auto.

POWWOW REMNANTS

Warm walnut seats crisscross braces,
piercing quiet warriorless patterns

against collapsible arena walls.
Red cardboard posters curl around past
performances; drawn back from
beer cans scattered about like fallen
braves, bent or flattened by unknown hands.
One head-split drum dropped under a chair
collects flies to barbecue stains.
Small sparrows have left droppings to be remembered by.

LANGSTON HUGHES

His poems, yellow, torn and fading,
lie in the pages of an old book.
I broke its back,
exposing fibered endings of Congo
rivers, Oklahoma nights and Cleopatra's hair
fraying onto Harlem streets.
Near the end of one wispy fiber
his Kansas grandmother gored Jazzonia
on the cross.
Early next morning,
I taped the book back together
for my sleeping children.

THE FLICKER

Some silent movie star
was murdered late yesterday.
He was an old newspaper story,

yellow, torn and fading,
I found years ago
under the kitchen linoleum.
I wonder,
with the silence of his moving lips
(colorless in the ear and the eye),
if his celluloid body jerked to a stop
on the screen of the Douglas Art Theatre.

PLAYING POCAHONTAS

Playing Pocahontas was Paula's weekend work.
At circle fires,
she squatted beside Old Knife's son
waiting for the visions to come.
Following Grand Canyon's rim
with eagle-less eye
lost her many friends.
But a green chevrolet spirited her away
while the Thunderbird and Fish fought
their endless battle
and no one noticed.

THE FLINT HILLS

An orange line splits the sky
up the creek
where a dead ant
lies frozen

in a pool of summer souvenirs.
Overflowing the flint hills
the silent snow melts
beside a muddy trail
slapped by deer hide
long before.
A tribeless brave,
running fast like a swaying coyote,
lost the night that morning
as he stopped to listen
for the prison helicopter.

PEYOTE VISION

Exploding before my very eyes,
the bells ring again, drowning out voices;
mingling with cannon blasts
and questioning yesterday's
big three-colored comic books and tomorrow's
word-blackened texts.
General Douglas MacArthur, with a daisy in his ear,
answers all my questions,
as he rides in a black limousine.
With wispy hair darting back from crowd winds,
he speaks and I forget what he says
to watch his head become an explosion
of dream daisies.

THE WOYI

In South Oregon the Klamath play
a breath-holding game.
The spot where a brave runs
out of breath and falls,
they call the "woyi."
Tribal elders tell of some
who ran for a mile before
they fell.

INDIAN LOVE SONG

The trouble was too much
with all the lying and endless scheming
to be where he was not,
to be where they were.
After all, he did not love them.
True, he wanted breasts and legs
and hair and that warmth.
But not love.
For when the final bed squeak
was through, they would know
more of him than he could allow.
Still, he searched his senses
for the feel of purple
or sounds of aching moans
and found his fingers grafted to their backs.

AFTER THE FIRST FROST

The door slam
echoes off the wood and brick walls
lining the broken mulberry lane.
Within my backyard garden
red streaked poppies die
after the first frost.
The milkman wants
his money for the bill.
But Ginger has the money
and she is gone and I have
never worried about those things.

THE URBAN EXPERIENCE   *Part One*

Bobbing with the crowds,
Big Bear tried on
his various Pottawatomi faces
while his life flowed
into gutters, walls, streets and passing breasts.
Kansas City sidewalks led him
to places where no grass grows.
His shadow passed his uncle's barber shop
where on a pea green wall,
stained from open shop days
when Indians wanted to terminate,
the cola clock was stopped
as the cord dangled down with no plug.

Big Bear walked down a narrow alley
where he could not spread his arms
their full length. He did not try.

THE URBAN EXPERIENCE   *Part Two*

Flying Horse was in jail.
Flying Horse sang he was so tired.
He was so tired of ripping flags
off short shiny antennas.
He was so tired of silent clerks
clipping prices at him
while a slick bologna bulged
in his back pocket.
He was so tired of bibles
belting around his Arapho head.
So one anxious evening, everso late,
in the cream white of his jail cell
he dreamed the midnight dancers
buried him head down.

WISGA*

Wisga walks at night,
troubling tobacco dreams
with rotting buttons in empty tea cups.
Spilling red bundles before
black bear's angry paws,
this devil trickster rapes unflown maidens

* Prairie Band Pottawatomi Indian mythological figure of evil.

LEW BLOCKCOLSKI

without fear.
Christ's drum hangs silent
and headless; no rains have come
since Spring.
Big Soldier's mountains are flat
without baptisms, choking on
yesterday's breath.
But no one blames Wisga
anymore.

MY DREAM

"I had this dream.
I was on the old town square,
holding a white man down.
My brother was nearby shouting.
I don't know what he was shouting.
Anyway, I was going to scalp this man.
Then I remembered I didn't know how to scalp.
I asked my brother. He didn't know either.
The man started to laugh and laugh and laugh.
I woke up."

THE 49 STOMP*

Bound in a moonlight circle,
arms locked in the sign language of love,
the band moves drunkenly around the camp fire.
I watch their feet and wonder
why no one ever seems to step on another.

* Prairie Band Pottawatomi Powwow Dance.

Carroll Arnett

(CHEROKEE)

THE STORY OF MY LIFE

Down there where I was
born and reared on

        Oklahoma red dirt,

a whirling wind came
out of the east, took

        me from the land

my grandfather drank
up, gambled away, land

        he stole from the Cherokee

woman he married—an
only memory of her in her

        near blindness scraping

the floral design on
her dinner plate—that wind

        carried me all the way

to California to dive-bomb
cigarette butts, to fight

        the Battle of Tijuana

whorehouses *semper*
fidelis, semper—another

north to go drunk, go to
school, study long-range

with a cold beer bottle
between one's legs, to think of

knowing that's as good as
you're going to feel all

the pure-dee truth of
a friend's saying,

who waits for someone
else to set him free—

to make a name (there stood
Jesus laughing to beat all,

got your work cut out
for you)—sentenced to

grant learneries by
way of Missouri at whose

had signed autographs
for 10¢ apiece, being

for his own self—then
back east to Maine

dry wind took me

genetic effects of driving

waking in the morning

day long, knowing

A slave is anyone

took me north

saying, man, you sure

upper midwestern land-

world's fair Goyathlay

allowed to keep half

where both the land and

those living on it are
too good to be true,

though progress throbs

all through the night—again
north among Ojibwe women

who still tell children,

"If ya don't be real real
good, Grandmother Spider'll

come down from Canada

and put medicine on ya."
Yet further on to Pig's Eye,

Minnesota, where at

the trials of Dennis and Russell
U. S. marshals wear

small green and yellow

diamond-shaped lapel pins
and get a hardon each

time the .357 Magnums

jounce snug against their
hips. Not wanting to

travel, I have traveled.

I have never been
a homeowner, have

always been a tenant,

will always be
a tenant and hold

as much as I can.

CARROLL ARNETT

179

ANADARKO JOHN

White buck come in
drunk in his red
and white inlaid
boots, found this

big Comanche man at
the urinal. Comanche
finished, zipped
up, started to leave.

"Saaaay, chief," holding
off the wall, shaking
it—"dint yo
mama never teach

you to wash yer hands
afta ya went
to the bathroom?"
Comanche at the door,

not looking back, says:
"Nom. But she
taught me not to
piss on my fingers."

REMOVAL: LAST PART

Walking eight hundred
miles of unheard-of

                              Alabama snow,

Mississippi blizzards
blowing themselves out

into the glaze

of Arkansas ice storms,
nine times they held

council to decide

they could only go
on, each stop counting

ten times ten

left dead in the snow,
throats leathered with

diphtheria, red

corn enough for just
the small boys. Four

thousand of the people

killed, another eight
thousand made it

to tell stories of

while they waited around
Fort Gibson and Oologah

for statehood, for

seventy years of dirt
farming, posing for

sepia half-tones, for

the mission schools, even
the insane asylum to be

divided up by

the Bureau and the Sooners
who again paid plenty

good money, for

strip mines and oil
money, weekenders

with Evinrudes,

the employment
office to open for

CARROLL ARNETT

1907 it ended
at Tahlequah and

toward another
new ending.

wine money. In

it goes on ending

LAND

Without this
what is
worth doing.

DRUNK

After what had
to be said was
almost said

so the distance
grew like a wall
of what is left

now I went to sit
in a room with
myself there being

nowhere else from
which I might
come back to you

as I did to find
you sleeping so
that what had

to be said right
then would have
to wait a while

longer there being
no hurry except
that afterward

I forgot what
I wanted and
had to say

and to this
end it seems
important

that it have
been said right
then though I

know there is
nothing gained by
hurrying to a room

or a wall to lie by
myself there being
nowhere else to go.

SOMETHING FOR SUPPER

> Only
the gray wind

CARROLL ARNETT

sings, sings of
what is around

the next corner
that I need

not wait for. It
will be there

ahead of me, long
before I am.

ROCK PAINTING   *for Will Petersen*

He works
stone to

what he
is made

of, not
soft though

not hard,
to last.

From his
hands, it

is in
the stone.

YOU

I

Without so much

as trying to look
the Mediterranean
Cherokee he is

a hurt out like

a shot of his own
choosing, to

walk toward
it

from a corner, any

place near
white eyes
or the goldenest

hair ever
seen. Listen,
what will you

keep, hold to

after the dark
settles: upon

a time way back
when animals

moved better than

stories of them
a blackness shining
far

off said I like
snow, it says
almost nothing.

CARROLL ARNETT

2

Then his wife

—"he'd done
the unforgivable,

married
a Protestant,

and never had a day's

luck since": a lesson
therein
for you not

against false gods,
rather that lust
comes home to roost—

then his wife

went bad,
ran away with

the children,
the dog, the cat,

each taking its

name along
for ease of
safe keeping,

something to
be close to
of a winter's night

turned colder.

3

A cat can have
kittens in an oven,

said Malcolm,
but that doesn't

make them biscuits.

Or he who saved
his used condoms
to strew around

elementary schoolyards,
calling it Adult
Education. You mean,

exclaimed

the interviewer,
you actually prefer

ah, wet dreams to
other forms of, ah

erotic experience?

Oh yeah, said
the minority
subject. But why?

Wellll,
I dunno,
ya meets a bettuh

class of people.

4

You are always
among the enemy.

I am not talking
paranoia,

I am talking

the second half
of the American
second century.

I am not unhappy
to be here, I am
happy to be

CARROLL ARNETT

not yet killed
anyone I know,

I am. For you.

at all. I have

and have good reason
to be proud of that.

Jim Tollerud

(M A K

EYE OF GOD

Sway song
Chant of the old
Breaths of ancestors
Whisper the shore
Rays of memories
Pass in aurora.
Grandfather speaks
of yesterday
The legend moonlight hunts.
Oh, morning
My spirit draws near you
The rain clears the air
and my heart feels
the sun.
Long ago the waves
were saltier
and the People strong.

EARTH

Down the coast south of here
Near the Ozette river
The raven breaks razor clams
Klock-shood   oh, klock-shood . . .
Past the giant red cedar
You will find the adz
Stuck in black rock
Guiding the trail of nettles
Spirit   oh, spirit . . .
Through the frog swamp
Listen for the blue jay
An omen of sight
Wait for the message
Week-seek   guide me now . . .
It has come
A light defracted bubble
Tools of the shaman
Medicine food.

WEEK-SEEK

From the land of refuge
I hear your voice
Echoing in the clouds
Just bring me near
The rain is calling
Nighthawk of wind
Hear the man speak
Wet and silent warrior

of vortex lodge
I come to bring silence
to grasp the time
And breathe your sweet
Behold our tongue
To wife and child
I worship the wind
Calm my thoughts
Of destruction and myth
Life is the kingdom
To you I pray.

BIRD OF POWER

Boom
The shrill whistle of the wolf
The steady pounding of buckskin
Boom
The first thunderbird appears,
Clad in blood, ash, and cloud feathers
Head and wing strike to the sun
Streaming over the rain-drenched hills
And musky,   salt ocean.
Then feeling the power of 5000 prayers
He dives into the raging winter ocean.
From the turbulent waters of morning mist,
Theu-kloots flies with strokes of thunder
To the west, in circles, over isle.
It drops the ebony blackfish
On the shell-beaten shore.

JIM TOLLERUD

Boom
The last pound of the drum.

BUZZ

Rumbling sound of man
Ear trouble from phono fan
Bring home magic dawn
Comet rumors across my lawn
Slipping past ghetto barns
Heading east around the stars
Picture, photo, visual woman
Yes,   I am, almost on quicksand
Cattle feast on the brush
Horses crunch and ice crush
Heartbeat continues, don't slow
Lovely raven lands on snow
Old lady angers 'cause of me
Engines hum and dog is free
There is room for us to be
Separately divided into three
Insect,   animal,   and human
Looming, fighting, waiting for you
Cold,   cold adrenalin wind
Ending thoughts of retrospect
The same moment rerun
This makes no sense?

ELEMENTARY

Wouldn't you like to know
Wouldn't you like to know
Wouldn't you like to know people
Come one,   come one
The time is right
Forget the world give up the fight
Not once I tell you . . .
We like the brew

RAINIER

Last time around the forest floor
Rain beating on the ferns
Red cedar roots stream with life
Mud puddles reach my shoes
The dust is wet and wind picks up
Country swept of mother guardian earth
Still, I am involved
Searching, searching for my liberty
Sunshine once again
Breathing rays descriptive
Odors of challenge bright motives

THIRSTY ISLAND

War canoes were ready,
Sleek, black

JIM TOLLERUD

193

Armed with whalebone clubs
The gray heavens
Drifted through the sleepy morning
Tears of Theu-kloots
Gently blessed the secluded island.
Sea and cedar smoke
Blended into a musky haze.
The sea now brushes the shore.
And from the tiny village
Sea warriors stir from their coarse sleep.
They garnish themselves in cedar robes
And depart the chilled island.

SUNRISE

The old canoe in
Frost of dawn
Gray water and
Black paddle combine
The man of age
Guides the small canoe
From hemlock village
Pray to the hunt
Morning is sacred,
The mind is refreshed
The hunt for food
Brings glory to the
Warrior of knowledge

King D. Kuka

(BLACKFEET)

FEBRUARY MORNING

I arose early and stepped outside
into a deep
ultramarine
morning.
As I walked to school, I gazed
toward a blue
morning
sky
and said, "I can walk."
I stopped at a twisted gray tree,
motionless in winter's guilt.
I stared through its empty arms.
Against the sky they superimposed a
geometric
design.
I said, "I can see."
Then I realized this crippled giant would
not awake in May.

Or in June.
Or ever.
I said, "I am alive."
    The last star winked at me as dawn
blew it out.
    I walked on and thought my way to class.

GALLERY OF MY HEART

Hanging on the walls
in the gallery of my heart
are endless scenes.
        Heaven within me.
        Time is forever.
"The Crucifixion." Pain shoots through me!
Electricity! I walk on.
"Hello, 'Mrs. Richard Yates.' How are you? Stern?
I bet beneath you're really very kind."
Kind as "Mona Lisa."
Smiling. Framed in gold.
I think, longer than an hour.
I wonder.
I tremble at
"The Third of May, 1808." Fears' sword slashes me!
Tension. Tighter and tighter.
Tighter still
until
"The Scream"!
I walk over to the "Breakfast Scene."
I yawn

Stretch. I doze standing.
    Reality in nothing.
    Hope in emptiness.
My feet disappear in thick red carpet.
Sculpture Room.
Ah! "The Kiss"!
So tender.
Loving. Invisible clouds of happiness invade the room.
A tear slides out of my eye and jumps
into the carpet.
"Pietà." Flesh and Blood in marble.
I am humbled.
I am awestruck.
I kneel.
And now with "Winged Victory"
grandeur and power,
I almost fly.
The arms of my gallery stretch on and on
forever.
    The blue room.
    The yellow room.
    Green.
    Violet.
Free your emotion prisoners to the wind.
Walk in, enjoy my treasures.

JANNA

Your blond hair and autumn sweater
melt almost into one
and melt into a pattern of warmth.

KING D. KUKA

197

Skinny-rimmed glasses frame
intelligent gray eyes
and I can see a lifetime into them.
You're tall and proud,
like a larch in September.
Your breasts are young.
They cover a heart
yet unbroken,
as I hope it will
always be.
Your dimples tell me
you are happy.
Isn't it strange
how being near you
makes
me
happy too?

MY FRIEND THE WIND

I will call you
Laughing Child.
You always seem so happy.
You caress my cheek
with tenderness and warmth.
Your friendliness is unexcelled,
you wave to the hills.
To the hawk you lend a hand and
you always return to visit.
I will ride with you someday
and we will fly to a very happy land.

Voices of the Rainbow

JACKIE

Meet me tonight
under a veil of moonlight and dreams.
Together we
will walk.
With our eyes
we'll converse.
Your eyes.
Your beautiful emerald eyes
tell me you understand.
I can see a universe into them.
You are so young,
so free
like a breeze.
So innocent.
I watch you flutter
away
like a beautiful butterfly
leaving a
lonely smile.

UNTITLED

Tiny baby, you're ugly.
Three days old, alone.
Mother?
Well, I guess she's left.
Tiny baby, you're warm.
Future?
California's the promised land.

Sleep well, tiny Gayle.
Love?
Loneliness kindles it.
I'll pray for you in your new home.
Gayle Marie, you're beautiful.

EVENING

I watched a laughing cloud
waving to me,
saying good-bye
as it floated east
on its way to nowhere.
I heard an eagle crying.
I napped.
I awoke to sweet sagebrush.
From this towering ridge
evening's rosy cheeks smiled
as night began to close its eyes.
A warm August breeze
kissed me good night
and I closed my eyes
knowing the sand hills were near.

MY SONG

Sitting, legs crossed, copper-toned old man
Chanting in low bass.
    "Ho aa Hey yah"

"Way ah Hey ah"
Black Wolf is singing to the morning.
    "Hey a̅a̅ ah Hey"
    "Way ah Hey a̅a̅"
He is singing to many years ago.
    "Hey ah Way Hey"
    "Way ah Hey a̅a̅"
The singing stops.
Drum silent.
Black Wolf looks down at his drum.
He has sung.

Harold Littlebird

(SANTO DOMINGO/LAGUNA PUEBLO)

FOR TOM NUMKENA, HOPI/SPOKANE

in the tall quiet pines of Washington
in all that stillness
there is a home!
where the Spokane River, like a long blue-green serpent flows
and the salmon run like a bright burning fire in the fall
that is where we were
in those blue-gray mountains on an early morn
being the sound and smell of hunting
I was there searching once more
a pueblo hunter in the still frosty forests of the
Spokane Reservation, near Wellpinit
on that mountain in the Northwest
a deer waits for me
and it must have been forests and mountains like these
that Chief Joseph, the man
loved and died for, with a broken heart
longing to live there once more—
people of the past live here now and

I humble myself before them, praying,
asking that I might be lucky today
and continue that thing that all Indians know
that strength in a people's eyes
deep like wrinkles in old men's faces
hearing my prayers, a deer waits there
in the morning light that filters through those
tall dark trees
my breathing is long and easy
like the round dance songs the people here sing
my feet step slowly,
my eyes scan the meadows as I walk gently
gently, like the women's part in dancing
then all my movements cease; I am not alone
on the far hill, turned away, but knowing I am here
he stands broadside, waiting for my song,
in that space in time behind my eyes
clearly now the mystery is played out
I raise the rifle, singing in my heart
asking that our breathing be joined as one
Boom! an echo like thunder fills the air
in answer to the clouds now building in the west
and there, in that moment, I found a home!
like the bullet's home deep in the chest of
the white-tail buck bounding
then stumbling and finally falling
he has surely listened to the song,
song that continues and is endless like
the Spokane River flowing beside this reservation
somewhere long ago this timeless learning
happened before, and long from now will happen again
bringing with it all the joy and roundness that is in

our people's hearts
thankful am I that I could know it last autumn
with you and your people.
Hau! Hau! Hau!

FOR DRUM HADLEY

oh thank you cowboy with four-wheel drive
for bringing us here
where the hills are worked by erosion
and the sands sing songs to the silvery clouds
where ducks form V's as they fly overhead
and short clear-cut whistles are heard as they wing on by
oh thank you cowboy, standing there
where yucca and cedar are everywhere you look
and the air smells thick of sage
oh thank you cowboy, with four-wheel drive
for sharing with me the breezes of the crisp winter sky
and walking the arroyos where every curve is rounded
by melting snow
and a lone cock pheasant crows in the distance
oh thank you cowboy, with your big white stetson and red
                                                    handkerchief
for being in this parched Chimayo land
where my rifle's voice makes songs against the ever changing
red rock mesas
oh thank you bearded cowboy
for tasting this day together
with its rocks and arroyos and stubby piñon trees
this is where we are cowboy and where we'll always be . . .
with the land

HAROLD LITTLEBIRD

oh thank you Drum
for bringing us home

MOTHER / DEER / LADY

doe of the mountains east
you came for the hunter/father
a young lion came to the mountain
searching for his heart
doe/mother he found that heart
in the lady that came home
deer/lady from the mountains east
bearer of hunter seed
hair flowing, Spokane sunshine smiling
you are my heart, my mountain thighs
open that I may rest in that warmth and love
I am a hunter
you are the lady of my lifetime mountain
doe/mother/lady from the mountains east
I love you forever, always and in all ways

ALONE IS THE HUNTER

alone is the hunter
who seeks only to kill
and not reach into
what he has taken
and accept fully
all that was given

IF YOU CAN HEAR MY HOOVES . . .

if you can hear my hooves in crisp autumn leaves,
see my blue-gray body of winter,
then you will know the songs in my heart
songs of my lion heart
pulsing steadily with my eyes
awaiting the deer dancing with my spirit
pray there is that strength in me to bring him home

COULD I SAY I TOUCHED YOU

could I say I touched you
or that this quiet brown feather that blows
in my hand is what you are
touch of fur
cry of a gliding hawk
no other way can it be
to know you as a soft, sweet rain
or the unswerving flight of an eagle on wing
thank you for beautiful thoughts
for being a part of me, somewhere in time

OH BUT IT WAS GOOD . . .

Oh but it was good to leave in the rain
with Bruce walking beside me
being with me in that space
we all shared that weekend

HAROLD LITTLEBIRD

and it was good to talk with him
of the Ojo things and see him
covered up in his jacket
so the rain wouldn't hit his eyes
and we heard coyotes, and doves, and two-ton diesel trucks
and saw speed limit signs and drunks from the "moonlite bar"
and we tracked wearily down that two-lane highway
back to Santa Fe

COMING HOME IN MARCH

partying by a river near Ellwood City, Pennsylvania
getting loud and high
keeping company with people I met
and empty cans of past party-ers
and broken glass
a song from numbed mouth coming out
weakly bouncing back through the quiet
we all stood by the tracks and laughed at my song
"hey little Indian, sing that again"
"yeah bird, again"
song building
louder, clearer
"that's far out, man" "you're all right, littlebird"
"yeah, far out, bird"
away in winter
when men of the pueblo, young and old
sing the season, and the village echoes
the heart-throb of the drum beating strong—
a wind in the trees
moon climbing high

Voices of the Rainbow

stars shining brighter and brighter through cloudless sky
singing my heart deep into the night
holding on, remembering
lump in my throat growing harder

PENNSYLVANIA WINTER INDIAN 1974

like a woman you've longed to make love to, and finally did
was the warmth I bathed in, wandering through your land
where the colors of Winter unfold before you like a rolled-out
                                                    blanket
and the winds make forests bow as they gently weave and spin
                                                    their songs
through the open valleys and endless rolling hills
yellow grasses that stretch wide and far against a pale blue sky
bordering the ever present forests of thin dark trees
of which I know no name and
clear running brooks and creeks that flow onward toward the sea
these are the faces of the woman I saw, her name, Pennsylvania
she sang to me in her sunlit days and I listened
hearing the life that abounds in her woods
the deer, the squirrels, each animal has a different song and
would take a lifetime to hear them all
but I remember most the sounds of her body moving
sighing, heaving, giving birth to Spring
ice in the rivers breaking into thousands of pieces flowing South
going home to the sea, and I too, like the rivers going home
flowing and running clean remembering the woman of the East
in all I've seen
going home to my people, where life is flowing and forever
like the unbroken stillness of a cold Winter night

HAROLD LITTLEBIRD

back to the country from which I came
back to the yucca, cedar and crooked piñon trees
but I will tell my people of this woman,
the country East, and I will say with song in my heart
"country beautiful, now behind me, in my eyes and
ever in my heart"
and they will know your land of which I speak and
they will see as I saw all the greatness and
sincerity of Pennsylvania, the woman who cared
for her children and me as one of her children
roaming, rambling and singing in her hills and
open valleys, bathing in all her beauty

GAA-A-MUNA, A MOUNTAIN FLOWER

Gaa-a-muna, a mountain flower
That is your name
A name from the mountains
A name for your Father to know you
A name that I'll call you
Gaa-a-muna, a mountain flower
With tender blue petals

HUMMINGBIRD

hummingbird
magenta-green and white
carrier of light and wind
from the south you came singing

a high shrill whistle weighted with rain
everywhere you flew the grasses bowed in prayer
and a greenness came to the land as your song was heard
your wings rushed the clouds
to bring sweet wet seed from the skies
and everywhere you looked was singing

OLD MOKE . . .

old Moke, if you could see these mountains all around
if the two of us could laugh with the pines,
if a dark Pygmy and a dark Indian could share the tears
of a rainbow, then it would be as when cloudbursts
flood the forest of the Ituri and scatter the happiness
of the BaMbuti to everyone, everywhere, and all who will
accept this universal prayer

WRAP ME IN BLANKETS OF MOMENTARY WINDS

wrap me in blankets of momentary winds
run soft rain fingers through my coarse hair
let unending earthly vapors excite my nostrils
bring seeds of sun to pollinate my naked awareness
through tit-like mountains
through clear running streams
in soft pine needle beds
in ascending hills and rolling grasses
bring clouds to clothe my body

HAROLD LITTLEBIRD

bring the fruits and berries of a thousand sunsets
that I may eat and shine within
shed leaves of warmth to make my bed
that I will always sleep with you and
together our spirits will make love and give birth
to the seasons

FOR THE GIRLS 'CAUSE THEY KNOW

good night, my two little cloud ladies
Elima, fat dark rain bearer
you are the echoes of summer
the flooding of rivers
the shaping of arroyos
the tears in my eyes
Chamisa, gentle misty lady rain
you bring a joy to the fields
the answer of prayers for the corn
the melons, the chili and me
my two dark children
carrying a sorrow and strength
bring to us the lasting peace
we all once knew
good night my children

IN A DOUBLE RAINBOW

in a double rainbow
lives the summer rain

Voices of the Rainbow

who brings the seed
to soak the ground
to make dry arroyos run
as singing summer floods

Ray A. Young Bear

(MESQUAKI)

THE PLACE OF O

i'm not without you.
it's such a warm day
to wake up to,
to still feel yourself
dreaming,
always ending up where
the dead wake unexpectedly
with the mourners
taking it naturally
until the one dead
loosens his blankets
and walks around,
peering into the looks
on people's faces.
there is no time
to think about the handless
baby who has eased itself
out from the black box.

the sipping sounds
he makes enters our house
and he quenches himself
with the water from
our cups.

at the funeral,
the dead sorts you out
from the rest and knows
you are only pretending,
tells you it is no
longer important
and sends you on
to another dream
of lesser importance.
my uncle's breathing
expands into the wood
on the walls of the house.
he wonders if my ride
with the night has ended.

the fear of your death
remains in the comfort
of my sleep.
you have taken this star
over the haze of warm stones
and now you return
telling us that the sun
has grown on your back.
i can't do anything.
my lungs are still black
from the fire.

all night i have taken
myself apart,
rearranging my shoulders
and legs with fire,
trying to please my head
who i have put in place
of the woman who sniffs
the air for your cousin's
blood, i can't take her
from the rest.
a woman's dream for her
daughter is much stronger
than your death.

WHAT WE CAN

the winter must be here.
everyone grows weary
as they change worlds
not knowing which to learn
or which to keep from.

my grandmother wears
her sweater even before
the day is halfway through.

she is thinking
of snow and the times
she will brush it off
the green rock.

the hungry dogs and how
they will look at each
other when they find
that the green rock
has no mouth.

the fire will eat
the food for her grandchildren
and her knees will numb
in the snow.

i rub my face
against the window
feeling the change will
never take place
feeling everything that
we are it's not enough.

THE PLACE OF V

a short day has grown
into the sky,
balancing itself
between our places
of breathing.
the thought of warm
roomlight has left me.
the thought of our
hands against the house,
measuring each corner
and each window
has left me.

RAY A. YOUNG BEAR

the snow melts on
the ground and the yellow
of corn appears in the eyes
of flying birds.
the food you left
for the wandering man
walks behind you.
the killer's car
sits under the sun.
its eyes skim over
the walls of the house
looking for signs that
will make it remember
but it doesn't find
anything except a boy
carrying a boy who keeps
on fainting, falling
into seizures.
from the fog, an old man
troubles his weak legs
to kick stones alive.
his moist face attracts
you, tells you to leave
the past alone.
you offer the comfort
of your finger to fit
around his finger like
a ring so that he may
look at it now that he
is walking away in his
father's hands in the form
of four sticks.

BEFORE THE ACTUAL COLD

the wall continues
to face the muskrat
asking questions
about the deaths
and creations he missed.
how the muskrat muddied
his hands.

the wall doesn't
accept it.
the wall hands me
a mask and i stand
in the smoke of my
morning talking
mother
twisting myself free
from the muskrat's
dreaming stomach.

the river mixes itself
into the pregnant seal
quite well.
my mother is in the swamps
digging for roots again.

from the sky a knife
appears and chips the frost
off the clouds.
a dog climbs down
on a cord of daylight.

the seals have already
arrived

RAY A. YOUNG BEAR

wishing to help my mother
with her harvest.
the seals dry themselves
by rolling in the sand.
although it's just beginning
to get cold they have left
the snow falling inside
the earth.

THE WAY THE BIRD SAT

even for the wind there was no room.
the wind kept the cool to itself
and it seemed that his skin
also grew more selfish to feelings
for he was like a window
jealous of the light going through
denied his shadow the sun's warmth
when being alone brought him
the cool.

the way the bird sat
dividing the weather through songs
cleaning the snow and rain
from the underside of its wings
was evidence.
in its singing the bird counted
and acknowledged the changes
in the coolness of the wind.
he somehow held the bird responsible
as it flew about taking in puffs
of air.

Voices of the Rainbow

often the image of blue hearts
in the form of deer crossed his mind
outdoing all magic and distortion
of the hummingbird who had previously
been the source of his dreams.
the bird who had tunneled
through the daylight
creating lines in the air
for the people in his dreams to follow.

now his thoughts took him out
into a cornfield where he felt himself
bundled up concerned about the deer
and their hearts.
the hummingbird who had been dodging
the all-day rain stopped
and hovered beside him
before it flew off
licking the rain from the trees.

having killed and eaten so many deer
it was wrong to blame his weakness
on the sun and wind.
to accuse anyone nearby he thought
was as foolish as the consideration
to once save his morning's spit
with the intention of showing it
to people as proof that his blood
and time were almost out.
he even wanted to ask
if it was possible to leave it behind
for worship but all this faded away
like the flutter of wings
he always heard shooting past

the shadow of his foot before it
touched the ground.

once his nose bled all day
and he saved the blood
testing to see if his notions were true.
he allowed the blood to run into a cup
until the cup collected.
toward evening he emptied
the cup in the yard
and just before the sun left
the standing forms of blood glistened.
when he woke he found
his blood missing.
his dog looked content with blood
along the rim of his mouth.
there was nothing but dark spots
on the grass:

the daylight was full and the birds
walked through his yard
speaking to each other
and sometimes gathering
around the area where he had set
his blood.

it was strange as he watched.
each time they walked away
from the area it was smooth
and directed.
in his mind it reminded him
of a ceremony and he left lines
on where each bird had stepped
where each had circled
what words it might have said

even the prayers it might have sung
and when the birds had sticks
in their mouths he saw singers
with their notched sticks.
their beaks moved up and down
the sticks making a rasping noise
and when they hummed
it was a song he knew very well.
he danced to the rhythm
as he watched from the window.
the birds had faces of people
he had met and lost
but there was one he could not recognize
its face was of a deer.
he felt puzzled licking the rain
from the trees.

Carroll Arnett: "Born in Oklahoma City, 1927, of Cherokee-French ancestry. Educated by twenty-one months in the Marine Corps and later at the University of Oklahoma, Beloit College, the University of Texas. Currently I try to teach writing and Indian Literature at Central Michigan University.

"I write poems, when I can, because it seems sensible to do so and wasteful not to. A poem has a use insofar as it shows what it feels like to be alive or what a person does to himself or others by being alive. I write prose because it is the hardest thing I know, and I like to do hard things. I try to please people, a few of them, when I can, but pleasing is seldom an end in itself. More often it is a means of living—with or without people—and living is the most important thing.

"Maybe the poem called 'The Story of My Life' shows it better than I can here."

Charles Ballard: "I am a lecturer in English at Idaho State University. I am a Quapaw–Cherokee Indian with a master's degree from Oklahoma State University."

Lew Blockcolski: "Son of Polish and Cherokee–Choctaw mixed-blood parents. Child of Oklahoma mixed cultural. Man of Indian and white torn loyalties. Employee of Emporia State College as Indian Education Specialist. Husband of beautiful red-haired woman. Father of two girls. In short, I am a survivor."

Peter Blue Cloud: "Turtle Clan, Mohawk Tribe, Six Nations. Born June 10, 1933, at Kanawake (Caughnawaga Reservation). Former structural ironworker; now a carver of wood and a writer. Was in Alcatraz occupation and from that edited the book *Alcatraz Is Not an Island*. Now write poems for *Akwesasne Notes* and do hide paintings and wood carvings."

Anita Endrezze-Probst: "Although I am Yaqui, I've lived in the Northwest for ten years. I'm presently finishing up an M.A. degree in English (Creative Writing) and working in both college and high school writing programs. My husband, Dave, is Karok."

Phil George: "I am a Nez Percé–Tsimshian (Indian name: Two Swans Ascending From Still Waters), a member of the Seven Drum Religion, Nespelem Longhouse; great-grandson of Chief Tawatoy. I love Wallowa, grandmas, wardancing, and frybread."

Janet Campbell Hale: "I was born on January 11, 1947, on the Coeur d'Alene Reservation in northern Idaho. When I was ten my family moved to Wapato, Washington, on the Yakima Reservation. I disliked school and did poorly in it. I didn't attend school at all the year I was supposed to have been in ninth grade, just began the next year in the tenth grade. I worked as a waitress, I picked cherries, apricots, peaches, stripped hops. I painted, wrote poetry, read serious books. In 1963, with a tenth-grade education, twenty dollars in my pocket, and a youthful optimism I now find amazing, I went to San Francisco to seek my fortune. Times were hard for a long, long time.

"In 1968, without ever going any further in high school, I took City College of San Francisco's entrance exam, passed, and began my college career. I had a three-year-old son by this time. I worked at a variety of odd jobs during this time. The following year I transferred to the Berkeley campus. I earned my undergraduate degree in rhetoric, did graduate work in journalism. I worked for a short time as an editor-trainee for Harcourt, Brace, Jovanovich, and I worked for one year in the Department of Native American Studies at Berkeley as an instructor of reading and composition. I am now a law student at Berkeley's Boalt Hall.

"My poetry, short fiction, and essays have appeared in about a dozen literary magazines, academic journals, and anthologies. My first novel, *The Owl's Song*, was published in April 1974 by Doubleday. I have another novel in progress."

Patty L. Harjo ("Ya-Ka-Nes"): "Seneca-Seminole, born December 29, 1947, in Miami, Oklahoma. Conservator of Anthropology, Liaison and Community Co-ordinator of Native American Affairs for the Denver Museum of Natural History, Denver, Colorado. Institute of American Indian Arts, Santa Fe, New Mexico, 1965–1969; University of Colorado, Boulder, 1969–1971. Vincent Price Writing Awards, 1968; published in *South Dacotah Review*, *Indian Historian*, *Amon Carter*, and *The Way*. My art, in whichever media I choose, has but one purpose: To create a better understanding between my people, the American Indian, and all who encounter it."

Lance Henson: "Cheyenne. An ex-Marine, a member of the Cheyenne Dog Soldier Society. Raised in Oklahoma by Cheyenne grandparents. A graduate of Oklahoma College of Liberal Arts in Chickasha, Oklahoma, in 1972. Presently in the graduate school of creative writing at Tulsa University. My interest lies in expressing the inner mythic being of the Native American, his God, his views, his spiritual participation in the contemporary society of his native land. My work has appeared in several magazines and anthologies, and my book of poems, *Keeper of Arrows: Poems for the Cheyenne*, was published by Renaissance Press in 1972."

Roberta Hill: "I am a Wisconsin Oneida. . . . just finished one year in Minneapolis working for Poets-in-the-Schools and plan on being in Rosebud, South Dakota, next year working for Sinte Gleska College."

King D. Kuka: "I do painting and sculpture, and in my high-school years I wrote a lot. Only recently have I begun writing again. My work appears in the anthology *Whispering Winds*, and my writing awards are listed in the *Reference Encyclopedia of American Indians*, in the Who's Who section. I'm currently living in Valier, Montana."

Harold Littlebird: "Born in Albuquerque, New Mexico, in 1951, I am of American Indian descent. I am a Pueblo Indian from the pueblos of Santo Domingo and Laguna in New Mexico. My time is devoted to two major fields of art, writing and pottery, and my work is recognized in both. In 1972 Sveriges Radio-TV 2, Stockholm, Sweden, produced a documentary film on living American Indian artists, and I was included in it, making pottery, singing traditional Indian songs, and reciting my poetry, which later was translated into the Swedish language. I graduated from the Institute of American Indian Arts in 1969. While at the Institute, I received a Special Award from the Scottsdale National Poetry Contest in 1968 and First Place in the 1969 Vincent Price Awards in Poetry. My work has been published in numerous literary magazines, including *The New York Quarterly*, *Alcheringa*, and *The New Mexico Review*. I am included in *A Directory of American Poets* and listed in the *International Who's Who in Poetry*. I live in Santa Fe, New Mexico."

Thomas Peacock: "Have published in *Dacotah Territory*, Winter 1973–1974. I am Anishinabe, which means 'original people' when translated down from Chippewa. Am an out-of-tune singer and left-footed dancer of Anishinabe. Married, two children (future wild ricers and singers); have one Indian dog, Indian car, and live on the Fond-du-Lac Indian Reservation. Presently am head honch of the Indian Youth Program in Duluth, Minnesota, which includes: juvenile delinquency diversion program; Anishinabe boys' group home; Bizindun Indian School."

A. K. Redwing: "Born May 25, 1948, Wagner, South Dakota. Vietnam veteran—sociology major. Admire words and thoughts of K. Marx, Richard Brautigan, and Buddha."

Carter Revard: "Part Osage on father's side; Great-great-grandfather Joseph Revard ran first trading post in Oklahoma (killed by Cherokees in 1821), married Osage woman. My stepfather, Addison Jump, is full-blood Osage (brother Addison, Jr., teaches math at Haskell). Uncle Woody Camp (mother's brother) married Ponca woman; my cousins Carter, Craig, Dwain, Kathy are strong in AIM—I was in Wounded Knee briefly in March 1973 where Carter was one of the leaders. My Osage name is Nompewathe ('fear-inspiring'). The name Carter comes from an outlaw uncle, about whom I have written a poem called 'Support Your Local Police Dog.' I grew up in the country, between Pawhuska and Bartlesville, in squalor and freedom, with six brothers and sisters and an occasional tornado to help us tear the house down. I learned where Doe Creek ran into Buck Creek, helped train greyhounds for a dollar a day, won a radio quiz scholarship to the University of Tulsa, a Rhodes Scholarship to Oxford, loved my Indian grandmother's frybread and meat pies, followed the wheat harvest north, took a Ph.D. from Yale, and begot four children. Once when fire let seventeen jackrabbits out into the coursing park we ran them down and put them back into the pens so we could course the dogs on them that afternoon; the metaphysics of this are simple but I do not yet understand the ordinariness. Therefore I would like the race to start again at age seventeen. While waiting for an official decision on this, I teach English at Washington University in St. Louis. In 1974–1975, however, I will be in Oxford looking at dictionaries."

Leslie Marmon Silko: "My family are the Marmons at Old Laguna on the Laguna Pueblo Reservation where I grew up. We are mixed bloods—Laguna, Mexican, white—but the way we live is like Marmons, and if you are from Laguna Pueblo you will understand what I mean. All those languages, all those ways of living are combined, and we live somewhere on the fringes of all three. But I don't apologize for this any more—not to whites, not to full bloods—our origin is unlike any other. My poetry, my storytelling rise out of this source."

Contributors' Biographical Notes

Jim Tollerud: "Native American of the Makah Tribe. Born in Clallam County, Washington State. Graduated with honors from Institute of American Indian Arts in Santa Fe, New Mexico. Worked with films at C.F.W.C.–Santa Fe and Public Broadcasting System. I am a free-lance cinematographer, photographer, contemporary artist, and poet. Worked with Larry Bird and Vine Deloria, Jr., in 16mm films. Enjoy Chevy Corvettes and gardening. Currently employed by Clallam County."

Gerald Vizenor: "I am a writer and teacher and enrolled member of the Minnesota Chippewa Tribe from the White Earth Reservation in Minnesota, where my family lived for many generations before moving to the city. I have written for newspapers and magazines, have worked as a community organizer and college teacher, and am now an editorial writer for the Minneapolis *Tribune*. My publications include books and articles about tribal people and several collections of original haiku poetry. My autobiography was published in the fall of 1974 by the University of Minnesota Press."

Anna Walters: "I was born in Pawnee, Oklahoma, September 9, 1946. I moved to the Southwest as a teen-ager and find it too much a part of me ever to leave it behind. I am married to a Navajo artist, Harry Walters (Na-ton-sa-ka). We have two beautiful sons, Tony and Daniel. (Pawhoes, we call them, since they are part Pawnee and part Navajo.) I like to paint as well as write. Both allow consistent examination and evaluation of oneself. In all the world, only this is important. But I cannot speak for anyone else, only myself."

Ramona Wilson: "I was born in 1945 at Nespelem, Washington, of Jessie Matilda Jim. Until I was seventeen, I lived by the Columbia River, but then I traveled to Santa Fe, New Mexico. The Institute of American Indian Arts was just beginning and there, by great luck, James McGrath became my teacher for a brief time. As it happened, if it weren't for him I may not have had poems in this book. That beginning of poems came from his own love of words, and the energy he expended with love. All before came to a point in that beginning, and all after, of necessity, have been built on that beginning. And we learn to voice our praises.

"I live now in Oakland, California, with my husband, my daughter, and the baby I now carry. More beginnings, each day."

Ray A. Young Bear: "I was born in Tama, Iowa, November 12, 1950, member of the Mesquaki tribe, formerly known as Sauk and Fox. Student at the University of Northern Iowa at Cedar Falls, majoring in art. Published in *American Poetry Review* and *Northwest Review*."